LEARNING BEYOND THE CLASSROOM

Chers élèves, chers parents,

Le *Compagnon Web Plus Express Yourself Plus 4* offre :

- des exercices de grammaire et de vocabulaire ;
- tous les audios et vidéos du cahier ;
- des exercices supplémentaires portant sur les audios et les vidéos ;
- une rétroaction et des résultats immédiats.

Dear Students and Parents:

The *Express Yourself Plus 4 Companion Website Plus* offers:

- grammar and vocabulary exercises;
- all the audio and video clips from the Activity Book;
- additional exercises based on the audio and video clips;
- instant feedback and automatic grading.

POUR VOUS INSCRIRE / TO REGISTER

❶ Rendez-vous à l'adresse de connexion :
Go to:
▶ **http://cw.pearsonelt.ca/eyplus/4**

❷ Cliquez sur "Register" et suivez les instructions à l'écran.
Click on "Register" and then follow the onscreen instructions.

Votre inscription est valide pour une période de 12 mois à compter de la date de votre inscription.
Your registration is valid for 12 months from the date of registration.

Code d'accès
Access code ▶ | EX12ST-STEAD-MONIC-FURAN-REPOT-PIPES |

Besoin d'aide? Rendez-vous à l'adresse: ▶ http://assistance.pearsonerpi.com
In need of assistance? Go to: ▶ http://247pearsoned.custhelp.com

W134600 (A34600)

EXPRESS YOURSELF plus 4

KNOWLEDGE AND COMPETENCY-BASED LEARNING

Philippa Parks

Tanja Vaillancourt

Cara Webb

PEARSON

Montréal

Managing Editor
Sharnee Chait

Project Editor
Tessa Hearn

Copy Editor
Elizabeth Lewis

Proofreader
Katie Shafley

Coordinator, Rights and Permissions
Pierre Richard Bernier

Photo Research and Permissions
Marie-Chantal Masson

Art Director
Hélène Cousineau

Graphic Design Coordinator
Lyse LeBlanc

Cover Design
Sylvie Morissette

Book Design and Layout
Pige communication

Illustrations
Josée Bisaillon (page 41)
Alexandre Couture (page 96)
Simon Dupuis (pages 118–120)

Acknowledgements
We would like to thank all the teachers who were consulted during the development of this project.

Credits
Unit 1
pp. 10–11 "A Man of This World" by Corneille, reprinted with the permission of SODRAC.

Unit 2
pp. 43–44 "Walk Like the Buddha—The Art of Slow Protest" by Mike Hudema, as appeared in Adbusters #69, courtesy of Adbusters Media Foundation.

Unit 3
pp. 89–90 "Girl Scouts: Reality TV causes mean girl effect" by Sandra Ecklund, courtesy of Sandra Ecklund, Web Producer, ABC News 4.

Unit 4
pp. 97–98 "Skinny Models Banned from Catwalk." Copyright 2007 Reuters. Reprinted with permission from Reuters. License number REU-2922-MES.

pp. 105–106 "Permanent Pigment: Future Regrets" by Anthony E. Wolf. Text reprinted with the permission of *The Globe and Mail*. Copyright © 2007 by Anthony Wolf PhD.

pp. 118–121 "Already Perfect" by Elisa Donovan from *Chicken Soup for the Teenage Soul II,* edited by Jack Canfield, Mark Victor Hansen, and Kimberly Kirberger. Copyright © 1998 by Elisa Donovan. Reprinted with the permission of The Permissions Company, Inc., on behalf of Health Communications, Inc., www.hcibooks.com.

Dear Students,

Welcome to a new school year!

Learning another language like English can be challenging, but there are many ways to make it fun. This book is designed to help you explore familiar topics in English: your friends, your music and your reality, but it is also designed to help you discover new ideas and to help you express yourself on a variety of topics that may not be familiar to you yet. We've included puzzles, games and challenges to make learning English as fun as it can possibly be.

As you explore each unit, you will learn new vocabulary, expressions, skills and strategies that will help you to understand English and to communicate more easily. We encourage you to take these skills outside the classroom and use them whenever you can: reading signs, labels and posters in English; watching television and movies in English; writing online and speaking in English with people who don't speak your language. Make the most of every opportunity!

We hope that this book inspires you to learn English and that English becomes a language you love to use. Good luck!

Philippa Parks
Tanja Vaillancourt
Cara Webb

TABLE OF CONTENTS

FEATURES

Let's explore the features of your book.

The First Page of the Unit

Each unit starts with a cover page that includes:

The title of the unit ·····················

The guiding question you will answer ·····················
as you complete the unit

A vocabulary activity to get you ·····················
thinking about the theme of the unit

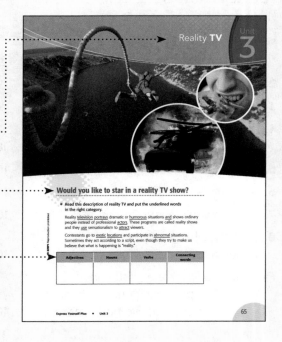

Smart Start ·····················

You begin with an activity
to find out what you already
know about the topic.

You will do a variety of activities
in each unit:

Speaking and communicating ·····················
with others

Smart Talk suggests ·····················
conversation starters.

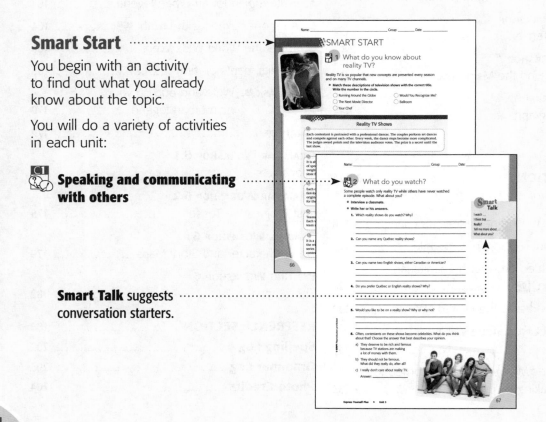

Reading and responding to a text

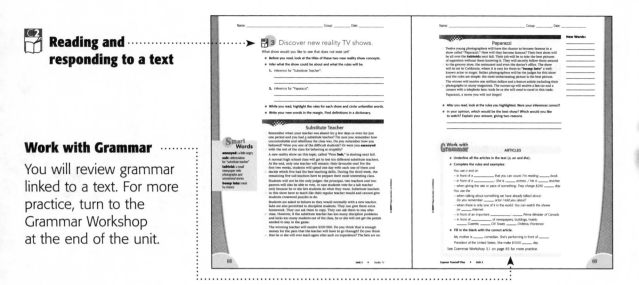

Work with Grammar

You will review grammar linked to a text. For more practice, turn to the Grammar Workshop at the end of the unit.

Listening and responding to an audio text

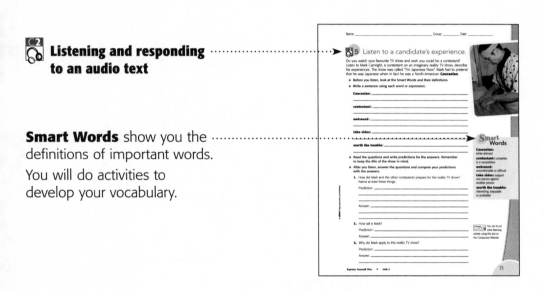

Smart Words show you the definitions of important words.

You will do activities to develop your vocabulary.

Watching and responding to a video text

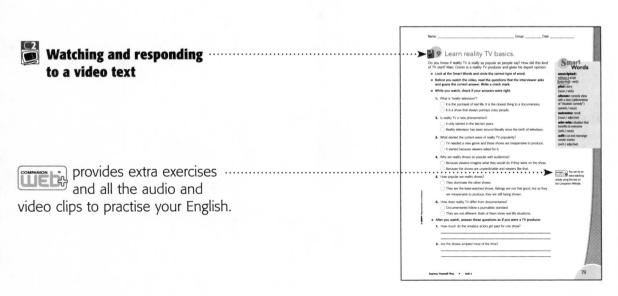

COMPANION **web+** provides extra exercises and all the audio and video clips to practise your English.

C3 ✏️ Writing and Final Task

You will have two opportunities to write. The Final Task can also be a production. The steps will help you do it right!

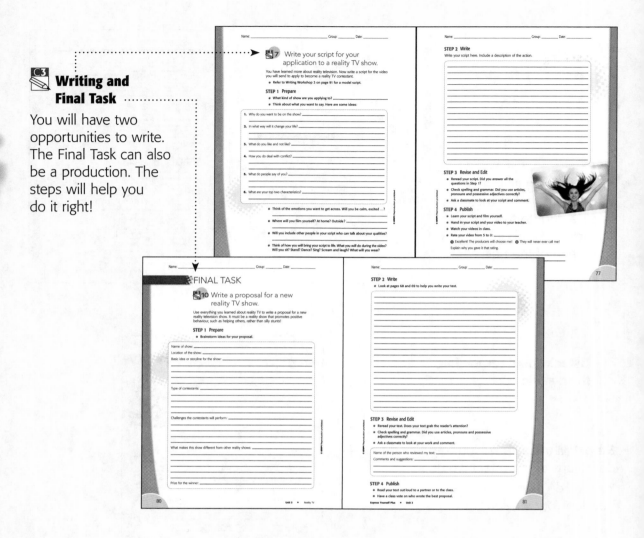

Wrap-up

This is the last page of the unit.

Test Your Smarts is a vocabulary game to review the words you learned in the unit.

Smart Expressions shows you two or three expressions linked to the theme of the unit.

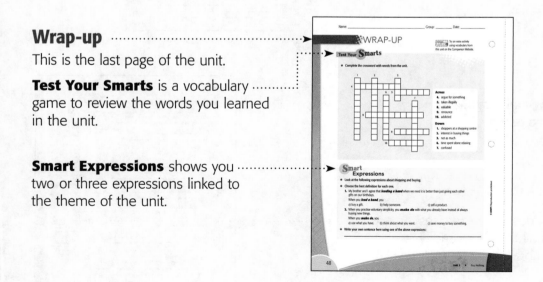

Workshops

Three kinds of workshops follow each unit:

Grammar Workshops show you charts and give you practice exercises on the grammar points you saw in the unit.

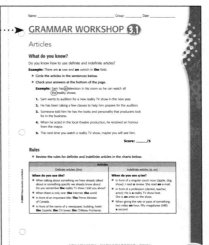

Reading Workshops focus on reading strategies and provide extra readings.

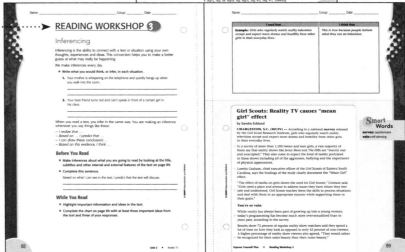

Writing Workshops provide instruction on the type of writing you do in the unit.

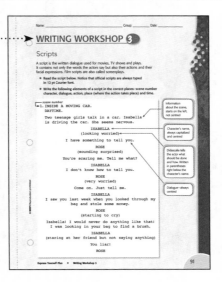

Reference Section

All the grammar charts are grouped together with the Irregular Verbs List, allowing you to refer to this section any time you speak or write.

Unit 1

Starting a BAND

How do you start a successful band?

Many people dream of becoming a famous musician. Do you?

- **Match the words to their synonyms in the word map.**

appearance	gig	make	write
create	invent	performance	

compose: *write*, __________, __________, __________

show: __________, __________, __________

SMART START

1 Start a band.

It is hard to find anyone in the world who does not enjoy music. Your taste in music reflects who you are and where you come from.

- **Read and answer these questions.**
- **Share your answers with a partner.**
- **Use Smart Talk to help you.**

1. What kinds of music do you like best?

_____

2. Name some bands you know. What type of music do they play?

_____

_____

3. What is the hardest part about being a musician?

_____

_____

4. What is the best part about being a musician?

_____

_____

5. Who is usually in a band? Name all the important positions.

_____

_____

6. Does everyone who works for a band have to be a good musician? Why or why not?

_____

_____

Smart Talk

I prefer … music because …

One band I know is …

The hardest part / the best part is …

2 Take the aptitude quiz.

Have you ever thought about being in a band? Take this quiz to find out how you could be most useful to your band.

- **First, ask yourself: What would I be best at in a band? Would I be a good manager? Would I be good at writing songs? Would I be good at advertising and publicity? Write your answer.**

_____

- **Read the quiz and circle your answers.**
- **Compare your quiz results to the answer you gave before taking the quiz. Were you right about your role?**
- **If you don't know a word, look at the sentence and guess its meaning.**

What's My Tune?

1	**Which of the following sets of adjectives best describes you?**	6	**Which activity do you prefer?**
	(A) Friendly and diplomatic		(A) Spending time talking with friends
	(B) Creative and quiet		(B) Reading or writing by myself
	(C) Outgoing and optimistic		(C) Creating a video or poster starring my friends and me

2	**How do you prefer to work?**	7	**How do you feel about rules?**
	(A) In a group—I like to encourage others.		(A) Rules should make everything fair.
	(B) Alone—I like to work on my own ideas.		(B) Rules should respect the individual.
	(C) It doesn't matter—as long as I am the centre of attention!		(C) Rules should be broken if necessary.

3	**When you have a problem, how do you solve it?**	8	**What is the best project you have ever done?**
	(A) I talk to everyone and try to find a solution for all of us.		(A) A project I worked on with friends
	(B) I write out my feelings in a song or a poem.		(B) A project I worked on by myself
	(C) I get angry and then laugh about it quickly.		(C) A project that is beautiful

4	**Which sentence best describes your qualities?**	9	**What do you usually do in a group?**
	(A) I am well-organized and get along well with others.		(A) I make sure everyone feels included.
	(B) I am thoughtful and imaginative.		(B) I wait until someone asks to hear my ideas.
	(C) I am creative and funny.		(C) I talk first about my ideas.

5	**What is your biggest problem when you work in a team?**	10	**Which of the following sets of adjectives best describes you?**
	(A) I make too many compromises—I let everyone tell me what to do.		(A) Reliable and dependable
	(B) I don't like to listen to others—my ideas are usually better.		(B) Creative and unique
	(C) I am more concerned with appearance than with quality.		(C) Successful and distinctive

Add up the points:

(A)'s = _____

(B)'s = _____

(C)'s = _____

Interpret your score

If your score is mostly A:

You are diplomatic and well organized, and you listen to everyone's ideas.

You would make a great MANAGER. The manager of the band is in charge of organizing gigs (places to play) and making sure that the band members get along.

If your score is mostly B:

You are very creative and good with language. You enjoy writing and working by yourself.

You would make an excellent SONGWRITER / COMPOSER for the band. Your original ideas will ensure that your band is unique.

If your score is mostly C:

You are creative and like to be noticed. You are good at creating posters and videos.

You would make an ideal PUBLICIST, the person in charge of the band's publicity and advertising. You will make sure that the band's name becomes well known.

3 Get together and find a name.

Now that you have a good idea about your role in a band, it is time to find other band members and decide on a name.

- **Refer to the quiz you took and check off your role in the band.**

  ◯ manager   ◯ songwriter   ◯ publicist

- **Find two people who have the other two roles to form a band.**

- **Write down the names of your band members next to their roles.**

  Manager: _____

  Publicist: _____

  Songwriter/composer: _____

- **Find a name for your band. Read the suggestions below for help.**

Tips for Naming Your Band

1. Think about using the word *the* in front of your band name; for example, The Beatles, The Ramones, The Guess Who, The Beastie Boys.

2. Look around at the labels on items, at the names of different computer fonts, at household objects; for example, "HD TV."

3. Find the nearest book; go to page 56, second paragraph, line 3, words 5, 6 and 7. That will be your band name.

4. Go to an online encyclopedia and skim through a random article. At any time in the article, stop skimming, close your eyes and point to a word. Select a few words around it (fewer than five words total), and that will be your band name.

5. Use an expression you've heard; for example, "Plan B."

6. Brainstorm together and then narrow down your list. If one of you dislikes a name, don't use it.

- **Discuss what name to choose for your group. Use Smart Talk to help you.**

- **Write down the name of your band and design a logo to illustrate it.**

… would be a good name.
I agree / disagree because …
I like … because
What about …?
What do you think?
First of all …
Are we finished?
Good job!

4 Watch an interview with young Québec musicians.

Clément, Eric, Rémy and Milène are a group of young musicians who play together in a band. Listen to what they have to say about their experience.

- **Before you watch the video, make predictions. Answer these questions.**

    1. How old do you think the musicians are?

    _____

    2. What instruments do you think they play?

    _____

> **COMPANION WEB+** You can try an extra watching activity that uses this text on the Companion Website.

- **While you watch, complete the chart with information from the interview.**

Members' names	Age	Instrument(s) they play	How did they join the band?
Clément			*Not mentioned*
	16		
	Not mentioned		

- **While you watch a second time, answer these questions.**

    1. What is the name of the band being interviewed? _____

    2. How many members are there in the band? _____

    3. What style of music do they play? _____

    4. What themes do they write and sing about?

    _____

    5. Why is reggae the perfect style of music to fit with these themes?

    _____

    _____

    _____

- **Write two more questions that you would like to ask the members of the band.**

    1. _____

    2. _____

5 Read tips about starting a band.

As with any project, the question is where to start. Wikis can be good resources to use if you aren't sure where to begin or of the steps involved in a task. This wiki gives the top ten tips to help you get your band started.

- Before you read, scan the text for Smart Words and any other words you don't understand.
- Write your new words in the margin. Find definitions in a dictionary.

Smart Words

wiki: a collaborative website that allows people to add, remove and edit content in text

bandmate: member of your band

rehearsal: practice

amp (short for "amplifier"): a piece of electronic equipment used to make music and other sounds louder

cover song: song written, performed and made famous by another band

gig: concert where musicians and bands play

chill out: relax

Wiki: Starting a Band

You don't have to study music for years to start a band, and you don't have to spend a lot of money on equipment. Starting a band is a great way to have some fun with friends while exercising your creativity and your brain, too.

❶ Get an instrument to play. Borrow a guitar or ask if you can use the piano at your school if they have one. Schools often lend out instruments, too.

❷ Learn to play. You will need some help. A quick search on the Internet will result in all kinds of tutorials to help you get started. Many websites also include videos, which is helpful if you are a visual learner. Perhaps a friend is taking lessons and can recommend a teacher. If you call someone about taking lessons, ask if you can take one trial lesson before you commit. Joining your school band is also a great way to learn an instrument.

❸ Find **bandmates**. A three- or four-person group is an excellent way to start. Talk to your friends (and friends of friends) to see who else plays music or wants to. You can also put up a sign at a local music store, coffee shop, bookstore and so on. Maybe other people in your area are looking for bandmates, too.

❹ Find a place to play. Many new bands practise in a garage, but when you are searching for **rehearsal** space, be creative. Maybe someone has a basement you can use. There are rehearsal studios with equipment like **amps**, drums and microphones you can rent. (In Montréal, it costs about $30 per hour.) Have a rehearsal schedule: pick a day and time and rehearse every week.

❺ Practise! Start by choosing a few songs that each of you likes to listen to and then learn the music and words before the first band rehearsal. If you are starting with **cover songs**, this will help you learn the structure of a song. Once you are feeling more comfortable with your instrument, you can also write your own songs.

❻ Create a song list. You and your bandmates will want to agree on songs that you all like and want to play. Have at least five songs you know well before you play in front of people at a "**gig.**"

❼ Think of a name for your band. Choose one together that you all like.

❽ Find a venue. Does your school have a talent show? Can you play at a friend's party? Is there a local band that you like? Ask if you can open for them sometime. When you are looking for a venue, don't forget that you can also organize your own party with friends and family where you can perform your songs.

▶

New Words:

▶

9 Advertise. Talk with other people about the band, create posters for your shows and set up a simple website about your band. When you are taking band photos, try different environments: in an alley, in front of a brick wall or in a field looking off into the distance.

_____

_____

_____

10 **Chill out.** It doesn't matter where you play, you are going to be nervous. Even if your music isn't very good yet, get your friends and family to support you.

_____

_____

_____

_____

- List the tips in order of their usefulness.

_____

_____

_____

- Compare your list with your bandmates' lists. Together, make a list of the five tips that the band thinks are the most important to get you started.

_____

_____

_____

Work with Grammar

SIMPLE PRESENT AND PRESENT PROGRESSIVE

We use the simple present tense for a routine or a general truth.

- Scan the text to find the sentences below.

- Fill in the sentences with the correct simple present tense verb.

  1. Starting a band _____ a great way to have some fun with friends.

  2. Schools often _____ instruments, too.

  3. Many websites also _____ videos.

  4. Maybe someone _____ a basement you can use.

  5. _____ your school _____ a talent show?

The simple present is also used to express likes and dislikes, for example:
Jim *likes* to play acoustic guitar, but Sarah *prefers* electric guitar.

- Ask your partner: Which instrument do you like best?

  She/He _____.

We use the present progressive tense for an action that is taking place right now.

- Scan the text for verbs in the present progressive tense and underline them.

- How do you form the present progressive tense? Write the correct order of the items.

  > a) the verb *to be* in   b) *-ing* ending   c) subject   d) the main verb
  >   the simple present

  Answer: _____

See Grammar Workshop 1.1 on page 19 for more practice.

6 Listen to an interview with a musician.

 You can try an extra listening activity that uses this text on the Companion Website.

Jon Stein is a musician and music teacher who also puts bands together for a living. We asked him about the most important things to know when starting a band.

- Listen to the interview carefully.
- Use the word web to help you organize your notes and ideas.
- Use your notes to help you decide if the statements below are true or false. If a statement is false, write a correction.

Positive aspects:
Spend time with friends
_____
_____

Difficulties to expect:
_____
_____
_____

Being in a band

Strategies for success:
_____
_____
_____

Smart Words

film score: music for a film

PA system: equipment that makes someone's voice loud enough to be heard by a group of people (short for "public address system")

theme song: music that is always played for a particular movie or television show

	True	False
❶ The best part of being in a band, according to Jon, is the cool factor. ***Correction: Getting to spend time with your friends and being able to play music together is the best part of being in a band.***		✓
❷ The hardest part about being in a band is the cost of buying equipment.		
❸ Jon started playing with friends from high school.		
❹ A band gets well known on the Internet.		

		True	False
5	You find places to play in the newspaper, then go down and talk to the owners of the bars and never take no for an answer!		
6	A band is like a family because sometimes you fight.		
7	Fights are always resolved by everyone talking and agreeing.		
8	A band should practise as often as possible, three or four times a week.		
9	You should start a band to travel the world.		

Work with Grammar

QUESTIONS

- **Read some of the questions from the interview asking Jon how to do things.**

  How do bands actually get together?

  How do they find each other?

  How do you find places to play?

- **Write a rule for making questions using *How*.**

  How + _____ + _____ + _____ + complement?

The interviewer also asks questions beginning with *What*, for example: *What instruments do you play?*

- **What are the *wh* words used to make questions in English? Hint: there are five.** _____

- **Write a question for each of the five *wh* question words that you could use in your own interview.**

  1. _____

  2. _____

  3. _____

  4. _____

  5. _____

See Grammar Workshop 1.2 on page 22 for more practice.

7 Analyze a song.

Do you know how to write a song? Look at the lyrics to a song by Corneille to find out how it is structured.

- Scan the text and circle all the rhyming words you can find.
- Draw lines showing which pairs of rhyming words go together. The first one has been done for you.
- Read the lyrics to the song.
- While you read, notice the structure of the song. Indicate the verses and the chorus. The first verse and chorus have been labelled for you.

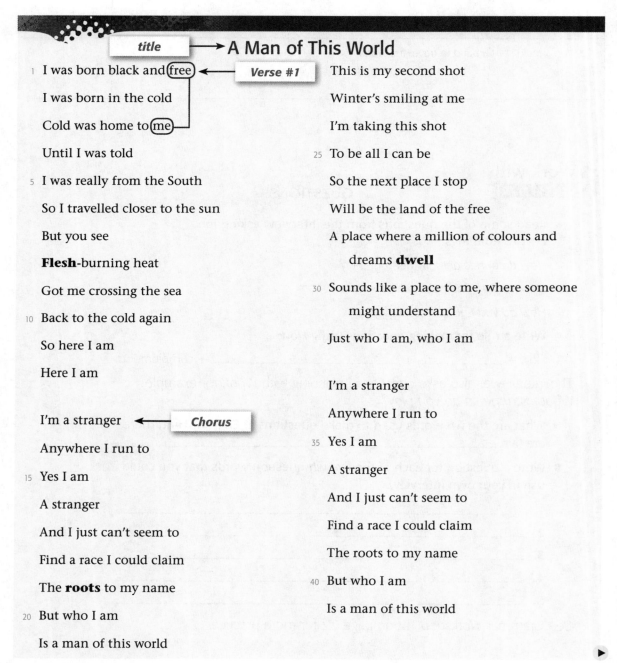

title → **A Man of This World**

Verse #1

1 I was born black and (free)

I was born in the cold

Cold was home to (me)

Until I was told

5 I was really from the South

So I travelled closer to the sun

But you see

Flesh-burning heat

Got me crossing the sea

10 Back to the cold again

So here I am

Here I am

Chorus

I'm a stranger

Anywhere I run to

15 Yes I am

A stranger

And I just can't seem to

Find a race I could claim

The **roots** to my name

20 But who I am

Is a man of this world

This is my second shot

Winter's smiling at me

I'm taking this shot

25 To be all I can be

So the next place I stop

Will be the land of the free

A place where a million of colours and

dreams **dwell**

30 Sounds like a place to me, where someone

might understand

Just who I am, who I am

I'm a stranger

Anywhere I run to

35 Yes I am

A stranger

And I just can't seem to

Find a race I could claim

The roots to my name

40 But who I am

Is a man of this world

▶ Now there's this **fuss** about colour

And everybody needs to belong

But take a minute to consider my perspective

45 You see, black kicked me out once

And white took me in

But white looked at me once

And nearly **spat** at my skin

I'm so confused, I'm so confused

50 About who I should hate

I figure I'll just love them all

Source: Corneille Nyungura, *A Man of This World.* SweetLyrics.com, n.d. Web. Feb. 15, 2012.

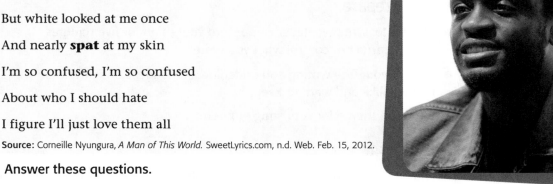

● Answer these questions.

1. What do you think this song is about?

_____

_____

_____

2. Where do you think this is: "… the land of the free, A place where a million of colours and dreams dwell"? Explain your answer.

_____

_____

_____

● Circle the best answer to complete the sentence.

1. If your **flesh** is pink or red,

 a) you have a sunburn or are hot.   b) you are cooking.

2. If you are researching your **roots**,

 a) you are learning how to plant trees.   b) you are learning your family history.

3. If you **dwell** in an apartment,

 a) it is where you go to school.   b) it is where you live.

4. If you are making a **fuss**,

 a) you are the centre of attention.   b) no one notices you.

5. If you are **spitting** on the ground,

 a) the ground will be wet.   b) the ground will be dry.

8 Write a song or lyric poem.

If you don't think you can write a song, try writing a lyric poem. Lyric poems have a song-like quality and can also be set to music. Use the model on page 10 to help you.

STEP 1 Prepare

- Free write: write whatever comes into your mind for five minutes. Do not correct or control what you write.
- Look at your free writing and underline all the ideas or sentences that you like and want to keep.
- Choose a theme for your song or poem.

STEP 2 Write

- Write a rough copy of your song or poem based on your free writing and notes.
- Try to use some rhyming words in either the chorus or the verses.
- Use the present tense correctly.

Verse 1: _____

_____

_____

_____

Chorus: _____

_____

_____

_____

Verse 2: _____

_____

_____

_____

STEP 3 Revise and Edit

- Reread your song or poem. Does it follow a structure? Do you have rhyming words?
- Check spelling and grammar. Did you use present tense correctly?
- Ask a classmate to look at your work and comment.

STEP 4 Publish

- Write the final version of your song on a separate piece of paper.

9 Spread the word.

Now that you have your band together and you have a few songs written, it's time to learn how to promote yourselves.

- Before you read, scan the text for unfamiliar vocabulary.
- Check the Smart Words first. If you don't find the word you're looking for there, look it up in a dictionary.
- Look at the Smart Words before you read.

Smart **Words**

spread the word: pass on a message

lyrics: words in a song

links: connection to another website

grassroots: ordinary people who promote something they believe in or enjoy

How to Promote Your Band

1 Figuring out how to get people to start listening to your music is one of the hardest parts of being a musician. You can be incredibly talented, play amazing music and get along really well with everyone in your band, but if no one has heard of you, they won't buy your music!

What can you do to promote your band and start **spreading the word** about your music?

5 One of the first things to do when you are trying to promote your band is to identify your TARGET AUDIENCE (the people who you think will listen to your band's music). If you know who you want to listen to your music and buy it, you will be able to create appropriate advertising. For example, if you are part of a band that plays children's music, your target audience will include parents. Parents read parenting magazines, so a parenting magazine

10 would be a great place to put an advertisement for your band.

Once you know who your target audience is, you need to identify what this audience WANTS or NEEDS. For example, parents want to know that their children will be happy and learn something when they listen to your music, so you need to make that clear by including information about how educational your songs are, or by printing up the **lyrics**

15 to your songs so that parents can read them and sing along with their children.

Think about how your band STANDS OUT from the others. What makes your band different? Unique? Better? For example, is your band an all-girl band? Is it a band that promotes a cause such as anti-racism? Make sure that you tell people all about why you are different!

Be creative when it comes to finding DIFFERENT MEDIA to promote your band. For example,
20 think about creating posters, videos, a website or band blog, T-shirts, hats or other articles for your fans to buy and wear. Start posting your music on the Internet. Make **links** from your website to other bands with similar musical styles and encourage other bands to make links to your website in exchange.

Where are the BEST PLACES to talk about your band? For
25 example, if your target audience is other teens, where do they go to listen to music? All-ages clubs? Talent shows at schools? Do they listen to a certain radio station? Do they go on specific websites? Once you figure out where your fans are, get a gig at that club, play at their schools, call up radio stations and ask them to
30 play your songs, make sure your songs are posted on that website.

Ask people who like your band's music to pass on the message for you. This kind of advertising is called **GRASSROOTS** because the message comes from the people who listen to your music, not the people promoting it! Encourage your friends and fans to write about
35 your band on their websites and to wear T-shirts or other clothing to promote your band.

- Apply the Smart Words to your own life by completing the sentences.

    1. We need to **spread the word** about _____.

    2. _____ writes the best **lyrics**.

    3. My favourite Internet **link** is _____.

    4. A **grassroots** cause I support is _____.

- Answer these questions and share your answers with your band.

    1. What are the five best marketing suggestions in the text? Why are they the best?

Marketing suggestion	Reason why it is helpful
❶	
❷	
❸	
❹	
❺	

2. Who is the target audience? _____

3. What is your target audience interested in? Give at least three activities or interests. _____
_____
_____

4. What different forms of media texts can you use to promote your band?
poster _____

5. Where can you promote your band? Write a check mark next to all that apply.

___ Internet   ___ newspaper   ___ street

___ magazine   ___ school

10 Learn the features of a poster.

- Read the features of a poster.
- Draw a line from the definition to the feature(s) on the poster.

Headline

The headline reinforces the poster's message.

Tip: Make it short (five words or fewer).

Visual

The visual part of a poster is the picture or photograph. It is the most important part because it establishes the message of your poster.

Tip: Use photographs because people are attracted to realistic images.

Body/Text

The body/text gives neccessary information. It comes under the headline. The sentences making the point of the poster and giving arguments appear here.

Tip: Keep the text short and simple.

Signature

The signature refers to the brand name, the logo or the name of the organization, company or creator.

Tip: Use bright or contrasting colours to make the signature stand out.

- Complete the left-hand column of the chart with information from the poster above.
- Complete the right-hand column with information for a poster for your band.

Things to include in a poster	Things to think about before making a poster
• An interesting visual: _two people dressed up_ _____	• Who is looking at the poster? _____ _____
• A clear topic/idea: _____ _____ _____	• What information do they need to know about the show? _____ _____
• A clear headline: _____ _____ _____	_____
	• What colours will you use to attract attention? _____
• Important information: _____ _____	• Where will you put the poster so it will be seen? _____ _____

FINAL TASK

11 Create a press pack to help you promote your band.

Each band member will create a media text to be included in a press pack that you can use to promote yourselves. Some media texts can be the same, but they should focus on different aspects of promoting the band. For example, if you choose to do two posters, one should promote a show and the other the band's latest album.

STEP 1 Prepare

- **Work with your bandmates to complete the chart so you know how each of you is contributing to the press pack.**

- **Read these media text suggestions to get you started.**

| poster for a show | band website | merchandise (T-shirt, band poster, stickers, pins) |
| poster for an album | album cover and song lyrics | |

Name	Media Text	Goal of Media Text

- **Brainstorm together for ideas. Look back at activity 9, page 14, to see what your group has already come up with.**

   1. Who is the target audience? _____
   _____

   2. What kind of music does your band play? _____

   3. What images and words will you include in your media text? _____
   _____

- **Working individually, write a plan or draw sketches of what you will do. Include details such as colour, size and relevant information.**

● Make a rough copy. For a poster, use a sheet of paper.

STEP 2 Produce

● Revise your work. Will it attract your target audience? Is your message clear?

● Check your spelling and grammar. Did you use the simple present and present progressive tenses correctly?

● Ask the other members of your group to take a look at your work and comment.

Name of one person who reviewed my text: _____

Comments/suggestions: _____

_____

● As a group, prepare a short presentation text that the publicity person can use to introduce your band and present your media texts.

Introduction: *Hello, everybody. Let me introduce you to (band and members)* _____

_____.

Body: *This band has worked so hard to put together an awesome (album/show/selection*

of merchandise) _____ *that we want to share with you.*

First, (name) _____ *will present* _____.

Then, _____.

After that, _____.

Conclusion: *We look forward to seeing you at our next show on* _____

_____.

STEP 3 Present

● Create the final version.

● Present your media texts to the class as a group.

WRAP-UP

Test Your Smarts

- Solve the cryptogram to reveal what lead singer Steven Tyler says about his band, Aerosmith.
- Note that the numbers are random and that you don't need to find all the letters of the alphabet.

A B C D E F G H I J K L M N O P Q

6 __ __ __ __ __ __ __ 7 __ __ __ __ __ __ __ __

R S T U V W X Y Z

__ __ __ __ __ __ __ __ __

A __   __ __ __ __   A __   I   A __ ,
6 16   2 10 10 18   6 16   7   6 21

I '__   __ __ __   I __ __
7   21   8 10 17 3   7 8 2

__ I __ __ __ __ __   __ __   __ A __ __ .
12 7 17 3 10 14 17   21 23   19 6 8 18

Smart Expressions

- Read the expressions and their definitions.
- Complete each sentence with the expression that fits best.

> **one-man band:** an organization in which one person does all the work or has all the power
> **play it by ear:** improvise, do what seems right at the time without planning
> **it takes two to tango:** Both people are responsible for the bad situation.

1. We couldn't decide which song to finish the concert with. We decided to _____ .
2. Chloe said Leo's lyrics didn't fit the song; Leo blamed Chloe's music.
   I said, "_____."
3. The reason our band broke up was because Eric loved to be in control of every aspect.
   He acted like a _____ .

- Write about a personal experience using one of the expressions.

_____

_____

_____

GRAMMAR WORKSHOP 1.1

Simple Present and Present Progressive Tenses

What do you know?

Do you know how to use the simple present and the present progressive tenses?

Example: I often **listen** to music. I **am listening** to music right now.

- Circle the correct form of the verb in each sentence.
- Underline the correct verb tense for each sentence.
- Check your answers at the bottom of the page.

   Example: Suzanne (wants / is wanting) to play in a band.

   <u>simple present</u> (P) / present progressive (PP)

   1. Jess's favourite band (plays / is playing) in town tonight.

   simple present / present progressive

   2. Phil always (buys / is buying) Jess tickets to concerts.

   simple present / present progressive

   3. Today, Jess (surprises / is surprising) Phil and (takes / is taking) him to the show.

   simple present / present progressive   simple present / present progressive

   4. Phil (doesn't like / isn't liking) surprises.

   simple present / present progressive

   5. Jess (is / is being) very excited about the show and the surprise.

   simple present / present progressive

   Score: _____/5

Rules

- Review the rules for using the simple present and the present progressive tenses in the charts below.

Simple Present Tense					
Monday	Tuesday	Wednesday	Thursday	Friday	Saturday

I **play** my guitar every day.

Rules	Examples
Subject + verb (base form)	He never **asks** for directions.
Add *s* for the third person singular	She **teaches** English overseas.
Add *–es* for words ending in *–sh*, *–ch*, *–s*, *–z*, *–x* and *–o*	

Key words: every day, all the time, usually, sometimes, often, always, never

Answers: 1-is playing / P; 2-buys / P; 3-is surprising, is taking / PP; 4-doesn't like / P; 5-is / P

Present Progressive Tense

Now

I **am playing** my guitar right now.

Rule	Examples
Subject + *to be* (base form) + main verb + *–ing*	I **am visiting** the museum today. They **are returning** tonight.
Key words: now, at the moment, today, tonight, soon	

Tips

● Choose the simple present tense for most actions in the present.

● Choose the present progressive tense only for actions that are taking place now or for definite events in the future.

Hint: When in doubt, use the simple present tense.

Try extra grammar exercises for the simple present and present progressive tenses on the Companion Website.

Practice

Exercise 1

● Complete the paragraph using the simple present tense.

Phil and Steve (play) _____*play*_____ in a band together. Phil (be) _____ the bassist and Steve (be) _____ the drummer. They (rehearse) _____ at least twice a week. Steve's dad (allow) _____ them to practise in the garage. His dad (support) _____ the boys and (want) _____ them to play a live show. Phil's parents (think) _____ Phil's music (be) _____ not very good. Still, Phil (ask) _____ everyone he (meet) _____ to join their band. They (need) _____ a guitarist and maybe a lead singer. They really (want) _____ a girl to join the band, but they (know, negative) _____ any girls who play an instrument. If you (hear) _____ of someone looking to join a band, (call) _____ Phil or Steve.

Exercise 2

● Answer the questions about you. Use the simple present tense.

● Circle all verbs in third person singular.

Example: Do you usually sing in the shower?

Yes, I (sing) in the shower. / No, I (don't sing) in the shower.

1. Does your best friend know how to play an instrument?

_____

2. Which band or musician do you like the most?

_____

3. When do you watch music videos?

_____

4. Does your best friend write music or lyrics?

_____

5. Do any of your friends play guitar?

_____

6. Is your mom's favourite instrument the piano?

_____

Exercise 3

● **Complete the story by writing the verbs in the present progressive tense.**

Terry (play) _____ *is playing* _____ a show at Ships and Chips Café tonight. Many of our

friends (come) _____ to watch the show. Terry (sing) _____

the songs that she wrote and she (dress up) _____ like a star. We (take)

_____ photos of her concert, which she (plan) _____

to post on her website. Her brother (film) _____ the concert, as well.

Terry (raise) _____ money to record an album. She (book) _____

a studio in Québec City as soon as she has enough money. We (support) _____

her because she has talent. It is important to support Québec artists. Musicians like Terry (work)

_____ hard to be recognized in Canada and around the world.

Exercise 4

● **Circle the correct verb tenses in the e-mail.**

Hint: You normally don't use the present progressive tense with the verbs *be*,
like, *have* and *know*.

Hi Sabrina,

I (am / am being) so glad to hear from you again. Music always (helps / is helping) me to
relax too. My best friend Nat and I (like / are liking) to dance whenever we (get / are getting)
a chance. We (try / are trying) to go dancing at least once a week. In fact, Nat (dances /
is dancing) right now!

I really (like / am liking) all kinds of music, but dance music (is / is being) my favourite.
I (hope / am hoping) to see Rihanna live during the holidays, but the tickets (cost / are costing)
a fortune. (Do you go / Are you going) to her show? Some people in our school (go / are going).

I (have / am having) to go now. My mom (yells / is yelling) at me to turn down my music.

Let's chat soon,

xo Christophe

GRAMMAR WORKSHOP 1.2

Questions

What do you know?

Do you know how to make information and yes/no questions?

Examples: How did he answer your question? Do you like asking questions?

● Match each answer to the correct question.

● Check your answers at the bottom of the page.

Answer		Question
Example: U2 and the Rolling Stones are classic bands.	f	a) Do you know anyone who plays in a band?
1. Seeing a band in a large venue with lots of people is the best.	○	b) What is your favourite style of music?
2. No, but I dream that someday I'll be a rock star.	○	c) Which do you prefer? Seeing a band in a large venue or seeing it in an intimate setting?
3. I know a girl from my class who plays drums in a rock band.	○	d) Do you play an instrument?
4. Heavy metal is my favourite kind of music.	○	e) How do you know if you have musical talent?
5. Learn to play an instrument and you'll find out.	○	f) What are the names of two classic bands?

Score: _____/5

Rules

● Review the rules for making information and yes/no questions in the charts below.

Information Questions		
Question word	**Refers to**	**Example**
Who?	a person	**Who** in your class plays an instrument?
What?	an object, a thing, a name	**What** is your favourite band?
Where?	a place	**Where** is your favourite band located?
When?	a time or a date	**When** does your band go on tour?
Why?	a reason	**Why** do you like playing music so much?
Whose?	a possession	**Whose** guitar are you playing?
Which?	a distinction	**Which** instrument do you prefer?
How?	a way, a manner	**How** do you learn to play so many songs?

Answers: 1-c; 2-d; 3-a; 4-b; 5-e

Information Questions
How can be used together with many adjectives:
How far? How big? How long? How interesting? How many?
How many is used for things you can count (friends, characters, problems):
How many people are there in your band?
How many songs do you know?
How much is used for things you can't count (sugar, coffee, money):
How much money do you make playing music?
How much time do you need to spend practising an instrument?

Yes/No Questions
There are two ways to form yes/no questions.

Verb *to be*	+	subject	+	adjective	=	Answer
Are		you		musical?		Yes, I am.
Is		your brother		a drummer?		No, he isn't.

Auxiliary	+	subject	+	verb	+	rest of the question	=	Answer
Do		you		like		country music?		No, I don't.
Does		she		listen		to that band?		Yes, she does.

Practice

 Try extra grammar exercises for questions on the Companion Website.

Exercise 1

● Complete each question with the correct question word.

Example: _____When_____ do you listen to music?

- a) which
- b) what
- c) when

1. _____ is the best musician in your school?

- a) what
- b) who
- c) when

2. _____ is the most interesting style of music?

- a) why
- b) who
- c) which

3. _____ does your band want to tour?

- a) whose
- b) where
- c) how many

4. _____ you think that touring with a band is easy work?

- a) do
- b) are
- c) why

5. _____ money do you think sound technicians make?

- a) how long
- b) how much
- c) how many

Exercise 2

- Match the beginning of each question with the correct ending.
- Use the Internet and research the answers.

Example: In which year (*d*)

1. What is the name ◯

2. Who won the award ◯

3. How long did Prince ◯

4. Are lots of new bands ◯

5. Which *Canadian Idol* singer ◯

6. Where does Elton John ◯

a) of the lead singer of Coldplay?

b) play during his show in Montréal in December 2011?

c) won the competition in 2008?

d) did the Beatles first appear on TV?

e) live?

f) for best new Canadian band in 2011?

g) getting contracts with record labels these days?

Exercise 3

- Write six questions to ask an aspiring musician using the question words provided.
- Exchange your questions with a partner.
- Answer your partner's questions as though you were an aspiring musician.

Question	Partner's Answer
Example: How *many lessons do you take a week?*	*I take one guitar lesson and two singing lessons a week.*
❶ Who	
❷ What	
❸ Where	
❹ When	
❺ How long	
❻ Why	
❼ How much	
❽ Which	

READING WORKSHOP 1

Each workshop focuses on a particular reading strategy or technique, asking that you practise your skills by reading a text. Have a pencil, highlighter and notebook available whenever you read.

Before you begin, take a minute to review the internal and external features of a text. You can use the questions in this chart as a guide.

Internal Features

1 What is the topic of the text?

The topic of the text is the main idea that is presented in the text

2 What type of language is used?

The type of language used in a text can be formal or informal.

Formal: May I help you?

Informal: Hey, what's up?

3 What are the text components?

Each text is different. Some texts have sections that are indicated using subtitles or numbering. Some texts include images or icons, while others use typefaces such as **bold**, *italics* or underlining to draw the reader's attention.

External Features

1 What is the goal of the text?

Knowing the purpose of the text helps you to understand it.

Your goal may be:
- to express feelings and opinions
- to inform
- to direct and influence
- to entertain

2 Who is the target audience?

The target audience includes the people who will read the text or be especially interested in it; for example, teens, adults or a specific group of people.

3 Which culture is reflected in the text?

Skimming and Scanning

In this workshop, you will practise two important strategies: skimming and scanning a text. You may not realize it, but you already skim and scan constantly when you read.

Let's look at skimming first.

You skim when you want to get a general sense of the topic and ideas in a text. When skimming, ignore the details and look for the main ideas. The main ideas in a text are usually found

– in the title;

– in the first and last paragraph;

– in the first sentence of each paragraph.

Before You Read

- **Practise skimming with the text below.**

  1. Look at the title.

  2. Read the first paragraph quickly.

  3. Read the first sentence in each paragraph quickly.

  4. Read the last paragraph quickly.

  5. Formulate a general idea of the topic of the text using the words and ideas you recognize.

While You Read

Check how well you skimmed the text.

- **Underline the statement that best reflects the overall topic and idea of the text.**

  1. How a band changed its members frequently

  2. How a band changed its name frequently

  3. How a band changed and evolved until it became famous

  4. How a band became famous

  5. How a band got its first recording contract

How One Band Began ...

In March of the year 1957, John, a sixteen-year-old student at the Quarry Bank School in Liverpool, England, decided to form a music group. He called his band The Quarrymen. There were six members: John, Colin, Eric, Pete, Rod and Ivan.

Musical influences

5 Their band played skiffle music, inspired by musicians from the American South. The instruments the band members used included guitar, drums, washboard and banjo. Later though, John became inspired by American rock'n'roll music and musicians such as Elvis Presley, Buddy Holly and Jerry Lee Lewis.

Band members change

10 In July 1957, The Quarrymen played in a gig in Woolton, a suburb of Liverpool. One of the band members, Ivan, invited his fifteen-year-old friend, Paul, to see them play. Ivan introduced Paul to John and the two immediately became friends. Paul joined the band soon after. John and Paul became the main songwriters for the group.

In February 1958, Paul invited his friend, fourteen-year-old George, to watch them play.
15 Now George joined the band as lead guitarist. Paul and John played guitar and sang. By January 1959, all John's school friends had quit the group on graduating from school. Only John, Paul and George were left.

Name changes

20 John was now studying art at the Liverpool College of Art. He invited his friend, Stu Sutcliffe, to join their band as a bassist. Stu suggested renaming the group The Beetles as a tribute to Buddy Holly and The Crickets. The band began to experiment with names. They called themselves The Beatals, Johnny and the Moondogs, Long John and the Beetles and The Silver Beatles. Finally, the band decided to stick with the name The Beatles.

Trip to Hamburg

25 Allan Williams, a friend of the band, got The Beatles a gig playing regularly in a club in Hamburg, Germany. Before they left England, they **hired** Pete Best as their full-time drummer. Many of the bands playing in Hamburg in the 1960s were from Liverpool.

For the next two years the group lived on and off in Hamburg, playing their
30 music. In 1961, Stu Sutcliffe quit the band and Paul McCartney took his place as the bass guitar player.

Smart **Words**

hire: employ someone for a job

Back in Liverpool

The Beatles were becoming more popular back home in Liverpool. They often played to full crowds at the Cavern Club. One night in November 1961, they met Brian Epstein.
35 Brian owned a local record store and wrote a music column in a local newspaper. He became the band's manager in 1962.

First recording contract

The band signed their first recording contract with the record label EMI. They began recording their first album at Abbey Road Studios in London in June 1962. At this point,
40 Ringo Starr replaced Pete Best as the drummer for the band.

First hit song

The band released two singles, "Love Me Do" and then "P.S. I Love You," in October 1962. "Love Me Do" became a UK hit.

The Beatles now had four members: John Lennon and George Harrison on guitar, Paul on
45 the bass and Ringo on drums. All four members sang, although Ringo usually sang in the background. John and Paul wrote all the songs.

This musical group, which had started as a group of teenagers in Liverpool, England, in the late 1950s, went on to become one of the most famous bands of all time.

After You Read

Scanning is almost the opposite of skimming. When you scan a text you are looking for a particular answer, fact, key word and/or idea.

When answering comprehension questions about a text, use scanning to find the answer.

- **Prepare to answer the questions by reading and scanning the text.**

    1. Underline the key words or phrases as you read the questions.

    2. Look for these words or phrases as you scan and underline them.

● **Answer the questions about the text using the words and phrases you underlined.**

Example: How many members were in the original band?
There were six members in the original band.

1. What kinds of instruments are used in skiffle music?

_____

_____

2. How did Paul and George join the band?

_____

_____

3. How old were John, Paul and George when they began playing in the band?

_____

_____

4. Who suggested renaming the group?

_____

_____

5. What were some of the names of the band? (Find at least five).

_____

_____

_____

6. Why did most of the original band members quit the group?

_____

_____

7. What did the band's first manager do as a job?

_____

_____

8. What was the band's first hit song?

_____

_____

9. Who were the final four members of this famous band?

_____

_____

10. Who wrote all the songs?

_____

_____

WRITING WORKSHOP ❶

The six writing workshops in this book are both a reference and a guide to help you develop your writing skills.

Lyric Poems

A lyric poem is a short poem that expresses personal thoughts and feelings about one specific topic or idea. Lyric poems usually have a rhyming pattern that is determined by the poet. People read lyric poems aloud because they have a song-like quality. In ancient Greece, poets sang their poems while playing a small harp-like instrument called a lyre.

● **Read the poem "Fire and Ice."**

Fire and Ice
by Robert Frost

	Rhyming pattern
Some say the world will end in fire,	A
Some say in ice.	◯
From what I've tasted of **desire**	A
I hold with those who favour fire.	A
But if it had to **perish** twice,	◯
I think I know enough of hate	◯
To say that for destruction ice	◯
Is also great	◯
And would **suffice**.	◯

Smart Words

desire: want
perish: die
suffice: be enough

Content

Take a look at the personal thoughts and feelings expressed in this poem.

● **Answer the following questions.**

1. What is the poem about?

_____

_____

2. What word does Robert Frost associate with fire? _____

3. What word does Robert Frost associate with ice? _____

4. Why do you think he makes these associations?

_____

_____

_____

Rhyming Pattern

Poets create rhyming patterns with the final words or syllables of lines of the poem.

- **Discover the poem's rhyming pattern.**

  1. Write A at the end of any line that ends in the word "fire" or in a word that rhymes with the word "fire."

  2. Write B at the end of any line that ends in the word "ice" or in a word that rhymes with the word "ice."

  3. Write C at the end of any line that ends in the word "hate" or in a word that rhymes with the word "hate."

- **What is the poem's rhyming pattern?** _____

Not all lyric poems have complex rhyming patterns.

- **Read the first verse of the poem "Putting in the Seed."**

  1. Write A at the end of any line ending with "tonight" or in a word that rhymes with "tonight."

  2. Write B at the end of any line ending with "see" or a word that rhymes with "see."

Smart Words

fetch: go and get something or someone

bury: put in the ground and cover with dirt

Putting in the Seed

by Robert Frost

	Rhyming pattern
You come to **fetch** me from my work tonight	A
When supper's on the table, and we'll see	◯
If I can leave off **burying** the white	A
Soft petals fallen from the apple tree.	◯

- **What is the rhyming pattern of this verse?** _____

Tip: When you read a poem with a more complex rhyming pattern, use the same technique. For each new rhyming pair, assign a new letter.

- **Write a word that rhymes with each word in the list in order to make rhyming pairs for a poem about a band.**

  Example: sing *ring* _____

  1. bang _____

  2. drum _____

  3. dance _____

  4. rock _____

  5. jam _____

Lyric Poems Versus Song Lyrics

One of the differences between a lyric poem and a song is that the song often has a chorus, which is a verse that is repeated. Lyric poems do not usually contain repeated verses but they can. A simple structure of a pop rock song is verse/chorus/verse/chorus.

- **Look back at the song by Corneille on page 10 in Unit 1.**

  1. What is the structure of "A Man of This World"?

  _____

Another structure used in pop songs is verse/chorus/verse/chorus/bridge/chorus.

A *bridge* is an optional change in the music where the lyrics and music are different from the verses and chorus. A bridge is never used in a lyric poem. A good example of a song that follows this structure is "I Want To Hold Your Hand" by The Beatles.

- **Look up the lyrics to another song by The Beatles. What is the structure of the song?**

  _____

- **Name another popular song that follows this structure.**

  _____

It's Your Turn

- **Write a lyric poem made up of two four-line verses.**
- **Keep in mind that a lyric poem is about your feelings and/or thoughts about a specific topic or idea. You are not telling a story here.**
- **Use the present or the present progressive as much as possible.**
- **Brainstorm a theme for your poem. Here are some suggestions, or you can choose your own.**
  - First date
  - Fast cars
  - Summer holidays
  - A messy bedroom
  - Another theme _____
- **Find rhyming words that fit with your theme. Write them below.**

  _____

  _____

  _____

- Write the title of your poem.

_____

- Write the first verse of your poem.

Verse 1: _____
_____
_____
_____
_____
_____
_____

- Write the second verse of your poem.

Verse 2: _____
_____
_____
_____
_____
_____
_____

- If you wanted to turn your lyric poem into a song, what would the chorus be?

Chorus: _____
_____
_____
_____
_____
_____
_____

- Once you have finished, go back and circle all your rhyming words.

  What is the rhyming pattern of each verse in your poem?

  – Verse 1: _____

  – Verse 2: _____

  – Chorus: _____

I BUY LOTS
OF THINGS
BUT CREATE
NOTHING

SORRY
WE'RE NOT
SHOPPING

END
CORPORATE
FUEDALISM!

Why should we learn to live more simply?

- Write as many brand names as you can think of in two minutes under the title "Brand Names."

- Write as many names of trees or plants as you can think of under the title "Names of Trees and Plants."

- Look at this list and compare your ideas with the person sitting next to you.

Brand Names	Names of Trees and Plants
Nike	*Pine tree*

:: SMART START

 1 Calculate your screen time.

What would you do if you had no electricity for twenty-four hours? We all spend a lot of time looking at screens of electronic devices; for example, computers, televisions and cellphones.

- With a partner, think of four activities you do using electronic screens.
- Write how much time you spend on each activity every day.
- Calculate how much time you spend on these activities every day, month and year.

Activity	Average time I spend doing this every day	TOTAL TIME
1 *sending text messages on my phone*		*Per day* = _____
2		*Per month* = _____
3		
4		*Per year* = _____
5		

- Answer the questions below. Write notes.
- Share your ideas with a partner or small group.
- Write a check mark next to the Smart Talk you can use.

Questions	My Thoughts / Ideas	Smart Talk
1 What did you learn from this experiment?		◯ I learned that … ◯ When I saw the total number of hours, it made me think about …
2 Do you think that you spend too much time in front of a screen? Why or why not?		◯ I believe that … ◯ Now that I know …, I could …
3 What could you do to change the situation? ***Should*** you change the situation?		◯ If we wanted to do something about this, we could …

2 Find out about voluntary simplicity.

Some people react to the stress of modern living by rejecting many modern inventions. "Voluntary simplicity" is the name that we give to the way some people choose to simplify their lives.

- Before you listen, circle the correct definitions for these Smart Words.

- Guess the meaning from the context of the sentence.

1. People are constantly in contact with one another and don't have any **downtime**.

Downtime is

   a) time spent with friends.   b) time spent alone.   c) time spent working.

2. People who practise voluntary simplicity reject **consumerism**.

Consumerism is

   a) an interest in buying things.   b) an interest in eating things.   c) an interest in knowing things.

3. People who **advocate** voluntary simplicity don't believe that we need to buy things to feel happy.

To **advocate** something means

   a) to criticize it.   b) to hate it.   c) to argue for it.

4. Take some time to figure out how to make your life simpler, easier and more **meaningful** through simple living.

Meaningful means

   a) valuable.   b) expensive.   c) difficult.

COMPANION **web** You can try an extra listening activity using this text on the Companion Website.

- While you listen, read the text.

- Fill in the blanks with the words that are missing.

Voluntary Simplicity

1   What does "voluntary simplicity" mean? Why are people interested in it? Who practises voluntary simplicity anyway? One hundred years ago, if you wanted to send a ___message___ to someone quickly, you could do only three things:

❶   Write a letter, mail it and then wait for the person to write you back and for the post
5   to deliver it.

❷   You could call them on the telephone and hope that they would be home (there were no answering machines!).

❸   You could go on your bicycle, a boat, a train or walk to where the person lived and _____ to them in person.

10   All of these ways of communicating took lots of time! Today we have _____ messaging, texting, e-mailing, blogging, personal websites, cellphones and many other ways to stay in touch with people—instantly!

   ▶

▶ We don't need a lot of _____ to pass on our messages, but on the other hand, we don't have a lot of time to "do nothing" either. People are constantly in contact with one
15 another and don't have any "**downtime**." The busier we are, the more stressed out we feel and the less time we seem to have. Many people react to the stress of modern living by trying to find ways to cut out _____ or live more simply.

Voluntary simplicity means choosing to live with only what is _____ for your spiritual, emotional and physical _____. That may sound simple, but
20 what does it really mean? Many people believe it means focusing on what really matters to you—spending time with people you love, exercising and eating healthy foods and even taking time to do nothing!

People who practise voluntary simplicity tend to reject **consumerism** and feel strongly about the environment and justice. They believe that _____ things cannot make you happy,
25 but that doing things yourself and with other people is what makes us truly satisfied.

People practise voluntary simplicity by consciously reducing the amount of things that they buy. When they buy less, they need to work less in order to earn less _____. People spend the extra time that they gain NOT working to buy things with their family or volunteering. Others may spend their extra free time meditating, exercising, playing music,
30 reading or pursuing creative activities such as art and crafts.

During the holiday season, people who practise voluntary simplicity give money to _____ instead of buying gifts, make presents for their friends and family or even spend time cooking, playing games or doing other activities that are more meaningful than giving a present.

People who **advocate** voluntary simplicity usually criticize _____ for encouraging
35 us to believe that we need to buy things to feel happy. They agree that cutting out, or cutting down on, television viewing is very important in simple living.

You may or may not agree with the idea of voluntary simplicity, but one thing is certain: it is a movement with a long history, and it has a long future ahead of it. Perhaps one day, when you are feeling stressed out and need a break, you will _____ the
40 television, computer, radio and cellphone and take some time to figure out how to make your life simpler, easier and more **meaningful** through simple living.

● **Answer these questions.**

1. Name three ways people communicated one hundred years ago.

_____

_____

2. What don't we have a lot of time for today?

_____

3. What happens when you buy less?

_____

4. What do people who practise voluntary simplicity do during the holidays? (Name three activities.)

_____

_____

5. Do you think that practising voluntary simplicity is a good idea? Why or why not?

_____

Work with Grammar

COUNT AND NON-COUNT NOUNS

- Circle the following nouns in the text on page 35.

simplicity	person	train	happiness
letter	telephone	time	justice

- Complete question 1 in the checklist below.

Checklist	Count Noun	Non-Count Noun
❶ Does it have an article (_____, _____ or _____) before it?		
❷ Does it have a plural form?		
❸ Can you count it (one ..., two ...)?		
❹ Is it a mass substance like rice, sand or air?		
❺ Is it an abstract idea like nature or love?		

- Write each of the nouns in the list above in the correct column in the chart.

Count Nouns	Non-Count Nouns
letter	*simplicity*

See Grammar Workshop 2.1 on page 49 for more practice.

3 Think about Buy Nothing Day.

Have you heard of Buy Nothing Day? During that day, people worldwide try to go the whole day without spending any money on anything—at all!

- Circle all the things in the box below that *you* buy on an average day.
- Underline all the things *you* use or participate in that are free.

affection	lunch	pair of shoes	song for my MP3 player
candy bar	magazine	sleep	water
clothing	oxygen	T-shirt	

- With a partner, cross off items in the box that are *not essential.*
  Use Smart Talk to help you.

- Answer this question: Could you go for an entire day without buying anything? Why or why not?

Smart Talk

I think that ... is not essential because ...

Why do you think we don't need ...?

If I didn't buy ... then ...

4 Read about giving up technology.

You are going to read an essay written by someone who decides to go without technology. She calls this "Going Unplugged."

- **Before you read, answer the following questions. Use your dictionary if you need to.**

  1. To *unplug* means to disconnect an electronic device from its electrical source. Why do you think the essay is called "Going Unplugged"?

  _____

  _____

  2. What kinds of things do you use every day that you "plug in"?

  _____

  3. What advantages do you think there are to being "unplugged"?

  _____

  _____

- **While you read, take notes in the margin.**

- **List all the things that the author will give up when she goes "unplugged."**

- **List all the things the author will gain when she goes "unplugged."**

Give up

- *episode of*
  her favourite
  television show

- ● _____
  _____

- ● _____
  _____

- ● _____

Smart Words

pocket: fold of fabric in clothing where you keep things

stolen (steal): taken illegally

hooked: addicted

less: not as much

give up: renounce

slice: piece

Going Unplugged

1　The other day I was taking the bus and I saw the strangest thing: a cellphone rang, and the guy who it belonged to reached into his **pocket**, took it out and threw it out of the window! I couldn't believe it! I don't know if the cellphone was his, if it was **stolen** or if it belonged to someone else, but the
5　action amazed me. I could never let my cellphone ring without answering it.

I am an addict. An electronics addict. I cannot spend a single day—OK, I'll be more honest, a single hour—without checking my e-mail, my cellphone, my home phone and the Internet for messages from my friends, family and, well, even from people I don't like!

10　Like almost everybody else I know, I'm **hooked** to my electronic world. Watching this guy on the bus made me think: How can I become **less** addicted?

That's when I started thinking about getting "unplugged." I am going to start simply: for one hour each day I will refuse to answer any phones, watch television, listen to the radio, turn on my computer or do anything else that
15　involves electronics. Maybe eventually I will be able to do a whole day every week. If that goes well, maybe I will be able to do one whole week every year.

Of course, just the thought of **giving up** my addiction fills me with anxiety: what if I miss something important? When I thought about this, I decided to see what was so important that I couldn't live without missing
20　it. I made a list: The latest episode of my favourite TV show. I could watch it again later on a re-run. A call from a friend. She will try again in an hour ▶

► if it is really important. A text message from my boyfriend? It will still be there in an hour. For every reason I could find to stay plugged in, I found another reason why an hour wouldn't make a difference.

25 Then I thought about this reason: What if there is an emergency in my family? OK, in theory, this could happen, although I still haven't gotten the emergency phone call at 3 a.m. that everyone seems to fear.

What am I going to do with my time instead of being plugged in? Well, for the first hour, I am going to read a book. The next day, I will meet a friend for a
30 cellphone-free coffee. Or I will take a walk with my dog. Or I will organize some of the family photos that are lying around. Or I will enjoy the sunshine in my garden. All of these options seem like a little **slice** of heaven. It should be great.

I wish now that I could meet that guy on the bus again and thank him for inspiring me to do this, although I still think he was at least partly wrong
35 to throw away his cellphone like that. He could at least have tried to recycle it.

Gain

- *time to read a book*
- _____
- _____
- _____
- _____
- _____
- _____
- _____
- _____

- Cross out the word that is not a synonym of the Smart Word.

hooked:	a) addicted	b) dependent	c) disgusted
give up:	a) begin	b) renounce	c) abandon
less:	a) reduced amount	b) increased amount	c) smaller amount
slice:	a) piece	b) portion	c) take
stolen:	a) taken illegally	b) returned	c) carried off

Work with Grammar

FUTURE TENSE

In the essay, the author makes plans for the future.

- Underline all the examples of the future tense you see.

- Complete these rules about the future tense.

    You can make the future tense in the following ways:

    1. by using the verb *be* + _____ + verb ⟶ I _____ *go to the gym.*

    2. by using _____ + verb ⟶ *She* _____ *see her friends tomorrow.*

- Read the following list of key words. Circle the ones that indicate the future tense.

    tomorrow   usually   next week   last year   in a few months

- Write a list of things that the following people will do tomorrow using the future tense.

    Tomorrow …

    1. I _____.

    2. my teacher _____.

    3. my parents _____.

    4. my friends _____.

See Grammar Workshop 2.2 on page 53 for more practice.

5 Plan your own essay about going unplugged.

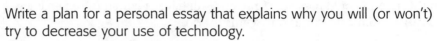

Write a plan for a personal essay that explains why you will (or won't) try to decrease your use of technology.

- **Refer to the essay on page 35 to help you.**

STEP 1 Prepare

- **Write notes about your positive and negative experiences with technology.**

STEP 2 Write

Start by writing an introduction paragraph.

When I was little, I thought that … Today I believe that …

_____
_____
_____
_____

Next, think of reasons for or against using technology. Write these in point form.

Helps us communicate. Saves time. Makes us too stressed out.

_____
_____
_____

Finally, summarize your ideas in a conclusion paragraph.

I really believe that … If we want to … then we should …

_____
_____
_____
_____

STEP 3 Revise and Edit

- **Reread your plan. Do you have a clear position? Do you support your position?**
- **Check spelling and grammar. Did you use count and non-count nouns correctly?**
- **Ask a classmate to look at your work and comment.**

STEP 4 Publish

- **Write the final version of your essay plan on a separate piece of paper.**

6 Learn about students against advertising in school.

Advertisements get you to buy a product by selling an image. They tell you that you will be cooler and more attractive if you buy the latest computer, the newest cellphone, a more expensive brand of shampoo and so on. Advertising influences us all to a greater or lesser degree. Should we limit advertising? Should school, in particular, be free of advertising?

COMPANION WEB+ You can try an extra watching activity using this text on the Companion Website.

See what some students at a school in Mississauga, Ontario, thought about it and what they did about it.

- Before you watch the video, answer these questions.
- Compare answers with a partner.
- Check the bottom of the page for the correct answer to the first question.

Questions	My Answer	My Partner's Answer
❶ How many advertising messages do you think you see or hear every day?		
❷ Where do most of these messages come from?		
❸ What is the goal of any advertisement?		
❹ Should schools be allowed to display advertising? Why or why not?		

Answer to question 1: We see anywhere from 250–3000 advertising messages every day.

- The first time you watch the video, take notes about the people you see using a character web. A character web can help you keep track of the people you meet in the video and the ideas and actions associated with them.

Against YNN

_____

_____

Dave Bran

Lori Pedwell

_____

Thought

_____

was suspended

_____

paper was against YNN

Lindsay Porter

Rod McDonald

_____

- **Watch the video again and answer these questions.**

  1. What is YNN? Why did the school want it?

  _____
  _____
  _____
  _____

  2. Why didn't the students want YNN?

  _____
  _____

  3. What happened when the students protested YNN? Give at least one example.

  _____
  _____
  _____

  4. Was the students' protest successful? Why or why not?

  _____
  _____

  5. How would you react if you were a student at that school?

  _____
  _____

  6. Do you know of any similar problems at your school? How can you make people (teachers, administrators, students) aware of the problem?

  _____
  _____
  _____

7 Discover a new way to protest.

People who participate in Buy Nothing Day and voluntary simplicity come up with some unique and interesting ways to draw attention to their cause. Read all about one group's experience in the next text.

- Before you read, find adjectives that describe the buy nothing / voluntary simplicity lifestyle.

- Write a list of adjectives that describe a busy shopping mall.

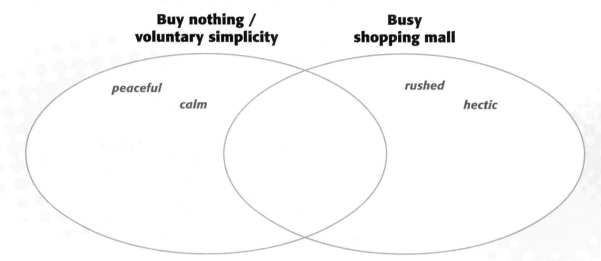

Buy nothing / voluntary simplicity

peaceful

calm

Busy shopping mall

rushed

hectic

- Compare the two lists. What do you notice? Do they have any words in common? Why or why not?

- While you read, practise saying the lines of the security officer (Security) and the activist (Us).

- Act out the scene a few times; try different accents for fun.

Walk Like the Buddha—The Art of Slow Protest

The "Buddha Walk" has its origins in a documentary movie in a scene where a monk is moving ever so slowly and peacefully through a busy New York city street. The idea was adapted for Buy Nothing Day in a large shopping mall—one of the world's largest—in Edmonton, Canada.

5 Four of us started moving in super-slow motion, one behind the other, as the busy **mall patrons** passed us by.

The action worked—shopper after shopper stopped to watch as we made our way from the **ground floor** to the main floor. People gathered, and many of them wondered out loud what we were doing and why we were 10 there. Some of them thought we were part of the local **fringe theatre** festival. Others remarked that we were simply strange; one person even suggested that we might steal something.

Eventually a mall security officer arrived to engage us in a conversation as we continued our slow progression through the mall.

Smart Words

mall patron: person who shops at a shopping centre

ground floor: first floor

fringe theatre: avant-garde or street theatre

▶

▶

Smart Words

flustered: confused

jeer: make fun of

sense of catharsis: feeling of relief

15 **Security:** You'll have to stop that or I'll have to remove you.

Us: Stop what?

Security: What you are doing.

Us: What are we doing?

Security: You are creating a spectacle.

20 **Us:** How are we creating a spectacle?

Security: Well ... uh ... you are walking very slowly.

Us: [slowly pointing to an elderly person moving across the mall very slowly] Well, what about her? She's moving very slowly.

Security: No, she's moving at the normal speed.

25 **Us:** Can you show us what is the normal speed? I mean, how slowly can we walk and still remain in the mall?

Security: [getting **flustered**]: No, you simply have to leave the mall. Leave the mall or I will call the police to remove you.

At that point, we left the mall. We didn't feel the need to press the issue
30 with the police department. But as we walked off, a strange thing happened. The crowd that had gathered started clapping for us and **jeering** at the security officials. These shoppers—primarily middle-aged people—were now applauding, partly because of the absurdity of the situation and partly, perhaps, because we all have a desire to stand up to authority and we get
35 a certain **sense of catharsis** when we do.

We live in a time when we all seem to be out of breath most of the time, running from place to place. The Buddha walk lets you take a much-needed breath. At the same time, the action breaks people out of their routines, which is one of the first steps to change.

40 And besides, it's one of the best actions for any old lazy day when you want just a little something to do.

Source: Mike Hudema, AdBusters Media Foundation, January/February 2007 issue 69, vol. 15, no. 1, Vancouver, British Columbia, Canada.

● **Answer these questions.**

● **Compare answers with a partner.**

1. What would happen to you and your friends if you tried "The Buddha Walk" in your neighbourhood?

_____

_____

2. Where would be an ideal spot to get attention?

_____

_____

3. How do you think that people would react?

_____

_____

4. Is it a good idea to try this? Why or why not?

_____

_____

8 Become an activist.

It is Buy Nothing Day. At the local mall, an activist and a shopping mall patron meet. Participate in this role play to see what happens.

- Read the roles for the scenario.
- Sit with a partner and choose roles.
- Take a few minutes to prepare. Choose the Smart Talk key phrases you will need and write important words or ideas to use.
- Begin your role play. Continue the conversation for as long as you can!

Scenario: Buy Nothing Day

Role: Jamie, an activist

It is Buy Nothing Day. With a group of friends you go to the shopping mall and protest. You have a sign that reads, "All the best things in life are free. Go home and hug someone you love." Convince the shopping mall patrons that they should go home today.

Smart Talk

Important Words/Ideas:

- ◯ What are you doing …?
- ◯ Do you really think that …?
- ◯ Why don't you try …?
- ◯ Maybe your mother will appreciate …
- ◯ Is it possible that …?

_____
_____
_____
_____
_____
_____

Scenario: Buy Nothing Day

Role: Taylor, a shopper

It is your mother's birthday today and you forgot to buy her a present! At the shopping mall, you can't find anything appropriate as a present. Just then, you see Jamie and the other protesters. Explain your problem to Jamie.

Smart Talk

Important Words/Ideas:

- ◯ That's a funny sign …
- ◯ I don't think you understand …
- ◯ Let me explain why …
- ◯ I am sure that …
- ◯ I will think about …

_____
_____
_____
_____
_____
_____

FINAL TASK

9 Write a personal essay.

You've learned about voluntary simplicity and anti-consumerism. Now write a short essay that discusses why you will (or will not) participate in Buy Nothing Day or voluntary simplicity.

Refer to the essay on page 35 to help you.

STEP 1 Prepare

- Will you participate in Buy Nothing Day or voluntary simplicity? Write your answer and a few reasons in point form here.
- Include important vocabulary words you will need.

_____

_____

_____

- Write a plan for your essay or use the one you made on page 40 of this unit.
- Include an introduction, body paragraphs and conclusion.

STEP 2 Write

- Write the first draft of your essay.
- Include the future tense.
- Use count and non-count nouns correctly.

Start by writing the introduction paragraph. Remember that the introduction paragraph introduces the main idea with an example, an anecdote or a question.

When I was little, I thought that … Today I believe that …

_____

_____

_____

_____

_____

_____

_____

_____

_____

_____

▶ Write your body paragraphs. Use the ideas from your plan. Expand each point-form idea into a short paragraph.

I can save a lot of money if I participate in voluntary simplicity.
Every day I buy … and it costs …

[paragraph 1] _____

_____

_____

_____

[paragraph 2] _____

_____

_____

_____

[paragraph 3] _____

_____

_____

_____

Finish your essay by summarizing your ideas in a conclusion paragraph.

I really believe that … If we want to … then we should …

_____

_____

_____

_____

STEP 3 Revise and Edit

- Reread your text. Does your essay clearly explain your opinion?
  Do you use good examples to support your points?

- Check spelling and grammar. Did you use the future tense correctly?
  Did you use count and non-count nouns correctly?

- Ask a classmate to look at your work and comment.

Name of the person who reviewed my text: _____

Comments and suggestions: _____

_____

STEP 4 Publish

- Write the final version of your essay on a separate sheet of paper.

∴WRAP-UP

Try an extra activity using vocabulary from this unit on the Companion Website.

Test Your **S**marts

- Complete the crossword with words from the unit.

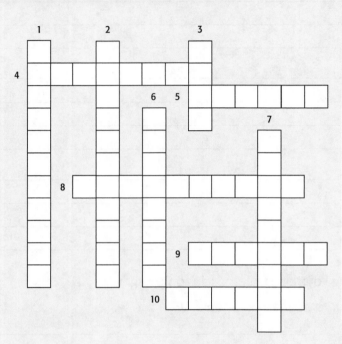

Across
4. argue for something
5. taken illegally
8. valuable
9. renounce
10. addicted

Down
1. shoppers at a shopping centre
2. interest in buying things
3. not as much
6. time spent alone relaxing
7. confused

Smart Expressions

- Look at the following expressions about shopping and buying.

- Choose the best definition for each one.

  1. My brother and I agree that **lending a hand** when we need it is better than just giving each other gifts on our birthdays.
  When you **lend a hand**, you
  a) buy a gift.   b) help someone.   c) sell a product.

  2. When you practise voluntary simplicity, you **make do** with what you already have instead of always buying new things.
  When you **make do**, you
  a) use what you have.   b) think about what you want.   c) save money to buy something.

- Write your own sentence here using one of the above expressions:

  _____

GRAMMAR WORKSHOP 2.1

Count and Non-Count Nouns

What do you know?

Do you know how to use count and non-count nouns?

Example: Money doesn't buy **happiness,** but it makes our **lives** easier.

- Complete each sentence with the plural form of the words provided.
- Use each word once.
- Check your answers at the bottom of the page.

~~book~~	tomato	child	potato	woman
handbag	piano	mouse	gift	music

Example: Pippa loves to read. She has many _____**books**_____.

1. Janet and her sister play a lot of wonderful _____ on their two _____.

2. We bought too many _____ for our spaghetti sauce.

3. We planted lots of _____ in our neighbourhood community garden, but they were eaten by _____.

4. Many _____ own too many _____.

5. Some _____ receive many _____ for their birthday.

Score: _____/5

Rules

- Review the rules for count nouns and non-count nouns in the charts below.

Count Nouns		
Most nouns in English are count. This means, you can count them. To form the plural, add the letter **s** alone or with other letters as shown below.		
Noun category	Forming the plural	Example
Most nouns	Add *s*	car ⟶ cars
Ending in –*x*, –*ch*, –*sh*, –*s*, –*z*	Add *es*	class ⟶ classes
Ending in –*f* or –*fe*	Change *f* to *v* and add *es* or *s*	half ⟶ halves
Ending in consonant + –*y*	Change *y* to *i* and add *es*	butterfly ⟶ butterflies
Ending in consonant + –*o*	Add *es*	echo ⟶ echoes

Name: _____ Group: _____ Date: _____

Exceptions			
Some count nouns are irregular.			
Singular	Plural	Singular	Plural
aircraft	aircraft	goose	geese
axis	axes	man	men
bacterium	bacteria	moose	moose
cactus	cacti	mouse	mice
child	children	ox	oxen
crisis	crises	person	people
criterion	criteria	phenomenon	phenomena
deer	deer	series	series
fish	fish	sheep	sheep
foot	feet	species	species
formula	formulae/formulas	tooth	teeth
fungus	fungi	woman	women

Non-Count Nouns	
Some nouns are *always* considered singular. These are called non-count nouns and you cannot count them.	
Category	Examples
Groups of objects	equipment, furniture, hair
Masses	rice, sand, sugar
Fluids	milk, gasoline, water
Abstract ideas	happiness, love, sadness

Try extra grammar exercises for count and non-count nouns on the Companion Website.

Practice

Exercise 1

- Circle the count nouns in each sentence.
- Rewrite the sentences using the plural form of each count noun.
- Conjugate the verb if necessary.

Example: The (child) was overwhelmed in the (toy store)
The children were overwhelmed in the toy stores.

1. The dog ran to the child.

_____

2. Mary made a donation by purchasing a sheep for her brother instead of buying a birthday gift.

_____

_____

50

Unit 2 • Buy Nothing

3. The woman donated a bag of oranges to the food bank.

_____

4. While the man was in the forest, he fished for fish, collected fungus and hunted a deer and a moose.

_____

_____

5. The sheep was in the field and the ox was in the barn.

_____

Exercise 2

- Complete the paragraph with the correct forms of the count nouns provided.

- You can use each noun more than once if necessary.

community	dilemma	gift	food bank
donation	charity	year	present
friend	person	family	

Example: Every year we shop for many ___*presents*___ for our ___*friends*___ and

___*families*___ . We always spend too much money, but we are also happy to see

how our _____ make others happy. It is a big _____ for us.

This year, we have decided to give _____ to local _____ such

as the _____ and the homeless shelter. We know that some people

would rather have a gift to open, but there are so many _____ in our

_____ who need help more, especially at this time of _____.

Exercise 3

- Decide if the underlined non-count noun is correct or incorrect.

- Correct any incorrect sentences.

	Correct	Incorrect
Example: We always buy too much <u>foods</u> for the holidays. So much is thrown away. *Correction: We always buy too much food for the holidays.*		✓
❶ Jill bought a lot of <u>furniture</u> at the store today. Her bedroom is too full now.		
❷ Mark didn't buy his grandmother any <u>jewellery</u> for her birthday. She asked him to donate to charity instead.		

	Correct	Incorrect
❸ Sandy would rather listen to <u>musics</u> than go shopping.		
❹ My dad has a lot of <u>patience</u>. My mother shops too much and he never complains about it.		
❺ Jim did his <u>homeworks</u> and then went for a long walk to clear his mind.		
❻ Sherry bought lots of <u>rices</u>, noodles, spices and vegetables. She likes to cook.		
❼ When we go to the ocean, we like to sit on the <u>sands</u> and watch the waves.		
❽ Jim likes to wash and comb his <u>hairs</u> first thing in the morning.		
❾ I have been lucky enough to have a lot of <u>love</u> in my life and not too much sadness.		

Exercise 4

- **Decide which of the words provided are count nouns and which are non-count nouns.**

- **Write each noun in the correct column.**

clothing	salt	flour	country	textbook	music
house	shirt	sugar	beauty	pencil	work
student	water	minute	world		

Count Nouns	Non-Count Nouns
	clothing

Exercise 5

- Circle the correct nouns in parentheses.
- Indicate whether the nouns are count (C) or non-count (NC) nouns.

A year ago, my family decided to simplify our (life /(lives)) __C__. We had too much (stuff / stuffs) _____. Instead of selling or throwing out our old (possessions / possession) _____, we chose to give them away. I had three (boxes / box) _____) of toys that I never played with and my sister had many pairs of (shoe / shoes) _____ that she never wore. My dad had a lot of old and broken (tool / tools) _____ and many jugs of (paint / paints) _____. My mom loves (purse / purses) _____, but we told her she could only keep three. She also had a few too many (skirt / skirts) _____. After we got rid of our (junk / junks), _____ we actually felt less stress in our lives. Now, instead of going shopping, we try to do something productive, such as reading a (book / books) _____.

Exercise 6

- Write a paragraph describing what you see out the window.
- Use as many count and non-count nouns as you can.

    Example: Looking out the window in the classroom, I see three birds on a tree.

_____

_____

_____

_____

GRAMMAR WORKSHOP 2.2

Future Tense

What do you know?

Do you know how to use the future tense?

    Example: I **am going to** the store where I **will buy** some food.

- Indicate whether the sentences are correct or incorrect.
- Check your answers at the bottom of the page.

Name: _____ Group: _____ Date: _____

	Correct	Incorrect
Example: The future tense is used to describe events that take place after this moment.	✓	
❶ Both **will** and **be going to** are used to form the future tense.		
❷ **Today** and **tomorrow** are **key words** to use with the future tense.		
❸ *"I am gonna to go to the shopping mall tomorrow."* is a correct example of the future tense.		
❹ **Will** is used to express prediction or an intention.		
❺ The correct contraction of **will not** is **willn't**.		

Score: _____ /5

Rules

● Review the rules for the future tense in the chart below.

Future Tense
When do you use it?
● To express a prediction: The protest **is going be** successful. People **will listen** to what we say.
● To express a plan: I **am going to spend** less money next year.
● To express an intention: We **will support** Buy Nothing Day.
Affirmative

Subject	+	will	+	base form of verb	+	rest of sentence.
I		**will**		**walk**		to school today.

Subject	+	verb *to be*	+	*going to*	+	base form of verb	+	rest of sentence.
I		**am**		**going to**		**walk**		to school today.

Negative (contraction)

Subject	+	will not / won't	+	base form of verb	+	rest of sentence.
I		**will not / won't**		**walk**		to school today.

Subject	+	verb *to be*	+	*not*	+	*going to*	+	base form of verb	+	rest of sentence.
I		**am**		**not**		**going to**		**walk**		to school today.

Question

Will	+	subject	+	base form of the verb	+	rest of sentence.
Will		you		**walk**		to school today?

Verb *to be*	+	subject	+	*going to*	+	base form of verb	+	rest of sentence.
Are		you		**going to**		**walk**		to school today?

Key words: tomorrow, later, next week, next year, today

Practice

COMPANION
ⓦⓔⓑ➕ Try extra
grammar
exercises for the future tense
on the Companion Website.

Exercise 1

- Complete the following sentences using *will*.
- Add the contracted form in the space provided.

Example: Sharon has a problem with shopping. She (need help)
_____*will need help*_____ during the holiday season. ·
Contracted form: *She'll need help*_____

1. She (spend) _____ too much money on gifts for friends and family.

Contracted forms: _____

2. She (buy) _____ too much food for Christmas dinner and most of
it (spoil) _____ and be thrown out.

Contracted forms: _____

3. She (receive) _____ her credit card bills in the new year and they
(be) _____ huge.

Contracted forms: _____

4 She (need) _____ to borrow more money to pay the bills.

Contracted form: _____

5 She (work) _____ half the year just to pay back what she owes.

Contracted form: _____

Exercise 2

- Unscramble each of the sentences.
- Rewrite the sentences in the negative (N) and the question (Q) forms.
- Identify what each sentence expresses (a prediction, a plan or an intention)
  in the space provided.

Example: life / will / ways / change / I / my / my / to / simplify

Answer: *I will change my ways to simplify my life.*_____

Negative: *I will not change my ways to simplify my life.*_____

Question: *Will I change my ways to simplify my life?*_____

Expresses: *an intention*_____

1. going / take / yoga / the / every / year / new / in / class / a / to / Monday / am / I

Answer: _____

_____

N: _____

_____

Q: _____

_____

Expresses: _____

2. will / reduce / spend / amount / money / I / I / the / of

Answer: _____

_____

N: _____

_____

Q: _____

_____

Expresses: _____

3. will / Sandrine / cut / up / tonight / credit / card / her

Answer: _____

_____

N: _____

_____

Q: _____

_____

Expresses: _____

4 am / dumpster / money / I / year / dive / going / save / to / to / this

Answer: _____

_____

N: _____

_____

Q: _____

_____

Expresses: _____

5. we / next / year, / instead of / will / donations / give / gifts

Answer: _____

_____

N: _____

_____

Q: _____

_____

Expresses: _____

Exercise 3

- Complete the sentences with the correct verb from the words provided.

- Use the future tense with *will* or *be going to*.

- You can use each verb more than once if necessary.

> serve   make   ask   help   be   have

Next week, _**I am going to be / will be**_ sixteen years old. I _____

_____ a birthday party. My dad _____

me prepare all the food. We _____

my friends some delicious homemade treats. I _____

my friends to make a donation to the food bank rather than buy me gifts.

As an activity, we _____ some cupcakes

for the kids at the women's shelter down the street.

It _____ a great day!

Exercise 4

- Write three ways you plan to incorporate the ideas of Buy Nothing Day into your life.

- Use the expression *be going to*.

Example: This year I am going to make my holiday gifts rather than buy them.

1. _____

_____

2. _____

_____

3. _____

_____

READING WORKSHOP ②

Taking Notes

There are three important steps for effective note-taking when reading:

– Skim or quickly read the text without taking notes the first time. Get a general sense of what the text is about.

– Take notes as you go through the text a second time, reading it closely.

– Write a summary of the text in your own words without looking at the text.

Before You Read

● Skim or quickly read the text without taking notes, to get an idea of what the text is about.

● Use the internal and external features such as the headlines, topic, audience, goal and language to help you.

1. What is this text about? Circle the correct answer.

a) volunteering   b) the environment   c) activists   d) buying things

While You Read

● Take notes as you read the text carefully.

● Underline or highlight the following:

– Main ideas

– Examples of these main ideas that help you understand them

– Unfamiliar words and/or definitions

● Put a number or asterisk (*) next to the most important ideas.

Smart Words

manifesto: written statement of beliefs and practices

sweatshop: factory where people work in poor conditions for little pay

padlocked: locked with a detachable lock hung on a hook

Anti-Consumption Activists

Author of *No Logo*

It's hard to believe that Naomi Klein loved brand names and shopping as a teen. It's also difficult to imagine this activist working at the mall, but this is what she did before she became a world-famous activist for change. Born and raised in Montréal, Québec, Naomi Klein is a Canadian journalist, activist and the author of several books, including *No Logo*. This book has become the **manifesto** of the anti-globalization movement worldwide.

Klein has visited **sweatshops** that have rules against talking and smiling, and places where the toilets are **padlocked** except during two fifteen-minute breaks each day, forcing workers who sew clothes for Western stores to urinate in plastic bags under their machines.

Because of Naomi Klein's work, people in the West are now demanding to know whether the companies whose clothes they choose to wear are following ethical labour standards. Klein is also helping workers who are paid only $2 for a shoe that sells in Canada for over
15 $100, in the hope that change will happen on both sides. Naomi Klein is helping us to think about how we want to affect the world next time we go shopping!

Founder of Adbusters

Kalle Lasn was born in Estonia and immigrated to Canada in the 1970s. He is the founder of *Adbusters*, an author and filmmaker and a leading Canadian activist in the anti-
20 consumption movement.

Lasn's documentaries and commercials have been broadcast on PBS and CBC as well as on stations around the world. He has won fifteen international awards for his work in film. He became an activist after he made a thirty-second ad on the **disappearing** old-growth forests of the Pacific Northwest and no television station would sell him
25 **airtime** to broadcast his commercial.

Lasn created the Adbusters Media Foundation and Powershift Advertising Agency to fight for the rights of citizens and activists to have access to airwaves. In 1992, he helped launch Buy Nothing Day. Even now, major networks such as MTV, Fox and CNN will not broadcast his commercials.

30 Lasn wants to educate the public. He believes over-consumption has major consequences on the environment. Everything that consumers buy impacts the planet in some way, from the packaging that is thrown into landfills to the sweatshops where goods are manufactured. Lasn also reminds people that the wealthiest nations, such as Canada and the U.S., consume 86 percent
35 of the goods on the world market, leaving only 14 percent for the rest of the world.

Smart
Words

disappearing:
ceasing to exist
airtime: time given
to an advertisement
on radio or TV

After You Read

- Put the text away.
- Write a short summary (50 words) of the text in your own words without looking at the text.

_____

_____

_____

_____

_____

_____

_____

_____

- Compare your summary to the text. How well did you understand the text?

_____

_____

_____

WRITING WORKSHOP 2

Essay

An essay is a short piece of writing on a particular subject. It has three main parts: an introduction, body paragraphs and a conclusion. Each of these main parts includes specific features. Let's look at the main parts.

Introduction

The introduction should be clear, concise and interesting enough to attract the reader's attention. There are three features of an effective introduction.

A Hook: The hook is an interesting statement, quote or question that presents the main topic of the essay. It can be one or two sentences but should always be brief and clear.

- **Write a check mark next to the best hook.**

    1. Can you imagine going shopping once a year and buying only the things you really need? ○

    2. In this article you will read about why it is important to buy fewer things. ○

- **Why is this hook the best? Write a check mark next to the correct answer.**

    1. It is short. ○

    2. It is in the form of a question, it is interesting and it presents the topic of the essay in one sentence. ○

B Thesis: A thesis statement is the topic of your essay.

- **Write a check mark next to the best thesis statement.**

    1. Living in a simple way is important for everyone. ○

    2. Studies show that voluntary simplicity is a way of living that reduces stress. ○

- **Why is this thesis statement the best? Explain.**

    _____

    _____

- **What is wrong with the other statement? Explain.**

    _____

    _____

C Preview: The preview is a sentence providing a brief overview of the information that will be covered in each body paragraph.

- **Write a check mark next to the best preview statement.**

  1. Voluntary simplicity is a trend that is growing in popularity and is very easy to do. ◯

  2. There are many ways to live more simply: by spending less, by spending more quality time with family and friends, by connecting with nature and by adopting a healthy lifestyle. ◯

- **Why is this preview statement the best.**

  _____

  _____

- **Read this introduction to an essay and identify the hook (A) the thesis (B) and the preview (C).**

> (A) Consume less and live more happily. ◯ Voluntary simplicity is a lifestyle people decide to follow for many reasons, including to reduce stress in their lives and to live more ecologically. People who practise simple living will choose a variety of ways to change their life. ◯ Buying fewer things, choosing to make less money and spending more time doing what they love are three of these ways.

Body Paragraphs

The body paragraphs develop the ideas of your essay. These are the ideas you gave in your preview.

When writing body paragraphs, introduce one idea per paragraph. Use facts, quotes and/or statistics to support the idea.

– Topic sentence: A good body paragraph begins with a strong topic sentence that introduces the main idea of the paragraph. The topic sentence doesn't have to be the first sentence, but it should be one of the initial sentences of the paragraph.

– Supporting sentences: These offer examples, definitions, reasons and/or evidence to support the main idea.

– Transition sentence: It is usually the last sentence in a body paragraph, and concludes the paragraph leading into the next paragraph.

- **Read Body paragraph 1. Underline the topic sentence(s) and circle the transition sentence.**

- **Write a topic sentence for the next two body paragraphs.**

Body paragraph 1: buying fewer things

A great place to start is by looking at your expenses. Take the time to figure out where your money goes and see if you can reduce your expenses. If you eat out for lunch every day, think about taking your lunch with you. If you have cable and you don't really watch TV, consider cancelling it. If you have a cellphone, think about getting the cheapest plan possible. However, voluntary simplicity is more than that. It is not only about money but also about working less so you have time to do the things that you love.

Body paragraph 2: choosing to make less money

Topic sentence: _____

_____

_____

Body paragraph 3: spending more time doing what you love

Topic sentence: _____

_____

_____

Conclusion and Extension

The conclusion must sum up all of the essay's arguments clearly and effectively. It consists of the following features.

A Review: This feature returns to ideas found in the introduction and summarizes the essay's main points.

B Extension: This goes at the end, after the review. It proposes a solution or reminds the reader why the topic is important.

- **Read the following conclusion. Identify A) the review and B) the extension.**

( ) Small changes will affect the way you feel, whether they involve going shopping less often, taking more time with your loved ones, going out for walks or eating fewer processed foods. ( ) These tips are just the beginning. If you want to learn more about voluntary simplicity, there are lots of books and websites that will help you on your journey to a peaceful, beautiful and simpler life.

- **Write a check mark beside the statement that best explains why the review is effective.**

  1. It has the same elements as in the introduction. ( )

  2. It gives you the same elements as in the body paragraphs. ( )

- Why is the extension effective? Write your answer.

  _____

  _____

It's Your Turn

- Write an information essay on one of the following topics or choose your own.

  1. Ways people can simplify their lives

  _____

  2. Activities that don't cost money

  _____

  3. Another topic: _____

- Organize your ideas into point form. Use the chart below to help you.

Introduction

Thesis: _____

Body paragraph 1

Topic: _____

Body paragraph 2

Topic: _____

Body paragraph 3

Topic: _____

Conclusion

Review: _____

_____

- Write a rough copy of the introduction.

Hook: _____

_____

Thesis: _____

_____

Preview: _____

_____

_____

● Write your body paragraphs.

● Write supporting sentences that explain or give more information about your topic.

Body paragraph 1 (topic: _____)

Topic sentence: _____

_____

Supporting sentences: _____

_____

_____

_____

Body paragraph 2 (topic: _____)

Topic sentence: _____

_____

Supporting sentences: _____

_____

_____

_____

Body paragraph 3 (topic: _____)

Topic sentence: _____

_____

Supporting sentences: _____

_____

_____

_____

● Write your conclusion and extension.

Review sentence: _____

_____

_____

Extension: _____

_____

_____

Would you like to star in a reality TV show?

● **Read this description of reality TV and put the underlined words in the right category.**

Reality <u>television</u> <u>portrays</u> dramatic or <u>humorous</u> situations <u>and</u> shows ordinary people instead of professional <u>actors</u>. These programs are called reality shows and they <u>use</u> sensationalism to <u>attract</u> viewers.

Contestants go to <u>exotic</u> <u>locations</u> and participate in <u>abnormal</u> situations. Sometimes they act according to a script, even though they try to make us believe that what is happening is "reality."

Adjectives	Nouns	Verbs	Connecting words

SMART START

1 What do you know about reality TV?

Reality TV is so popular that new concepts are presented every season and on many TV channels.

- **Match these descriptions of television shows with the correct title. Write the number in the circle.**

  ◯ Running Around the Globe   ◯ Would You Recognize Me?

  ◯ The Next Movie Director   ◯ Ballroom

  ◯ Your Chef

Reality TV Shows

Each contestant is partnered with a professional dancer. The couples perform set dances and compete against each other. Every week, the dance steps become more complicated. The judges award points and the television audience votes. The prize is a secret until the last show.

It is about overweight contestants trying to lose the most kilos with the help of a team of specialists. Every month two participants are eliminated: the one who lost the least weight and the one who did not exercise enough. The prize is free food at a health food store for ten years.

Each chef must invent five different recipes with the same ingredients. Diners at a fast-food restaurant become the judges, and they give points for flavour, presentation, originality and cost of the dish. Participants can also give points, but they cannot vote for themselves. The prize is the opening of a new restaurant.

Teams of four must face various challenges and perform certain tasks around the world. Each week, the slowest participants are eliminated from the competition until just one team remains. This team receives a prize of $100 000.

It is a performance competition to discover the best actor. The television viewers determine the winner. They vote for their favourite contestants, by telephone, Internet or text. The series has a panel of judges who critique the performances. There is no money prize, but contestants become instant stars.

2 What do you watch?

Some people watch only reality TV while others have never watched
a complete episode. What about you?

- **Interview a classmate.**

- **Write her or his answers.**

1. Which reality shows do you watch? Why?

_____

_____

_____

2. Can you name any Québec reality shows?

_____

_____

_____

3. Can you name two English shows, either Canadian or American?

_____

_____

_____

4. Do you prefer Québec or English reality shows? Why?

_____

_____

_____

5. Would you like to be on a reality show? Why or why not?

_____

_____

_____

6. Often, contestants on these shows become celebrities. What do you think
about that? Choose the answer that best describes your opinion.

a) They deserve to be rich and famous
   because TV stations are making
   a lot of money with them.

b) They should not be famous.
   What did they really do, after all?

c) I really don't care about reality TV.

   Answer: _____

Smart
  Talk

I watch …
I think that …
Really?
Tell me more about …
What about you?

3 Discover new reality TV shows.

What show would you like to see that does not exist yet?

- Before you read, look at the titles of these two new reality show concepts.
- Infer what the show could be about and what the rules will be.

   1. Inference for "Substitute Teacher":

   _____

   _____

   2. Inference for "Paparazzi":

   _____

   _____

- While you read, highlight the rules for each show and circle unfamiliar words.
- Write your new words in the margin. Find definitions in a dictionary.

Smart Words

annoyed: a little angry

sub: abbreviation for "substitute teacher"

tabloid: a small newspaper with photographs and sensational stories

bump into: meet by chance

Substitute Teacher

1 Remember when your teacher was absent for a few days or even for just one period and you had a substitute teacher? I'm sure you remember how uncontrollable and rebellious the class was. Do you remember how you behaved? Were you one of the difficult students? Or were you **annoyed**
5 with the rest of the class for behaving so stupidly?

A new reality show on this topic, called "Poor **Sub**," is starting next fall.

A normal high school class will get to test ten different substitute teachers. At the end, only one teacher will remain: their favourite one! For the first two weeks, students will spend one day with each one of them and
10 decide which five had the best teaching skills. During the third week, the remaining five sub teachers have to prepare their most interesting class.

Students will not be the only judges: the principal, two teachers and two parents will also be able to vote, in case students vote for a sub teacher only because he or she lets students do what they want. Substitute teachers
15 in this show have to teach like their regular teacher would and cannot give students crossword puzzles to do.

Students are asked to behave as they would normally with a new teacher. Subs are also permitted to discipline students. They can give them extra homework. They can ask them to copy. They can ask them to stay after
20 class. However, if the substitute teacher has too many discipline problems and kicks too many students out of the class, he or she will not get the points needed to stay in the game.

The winning teacher will receive $100 000. Do you think that is enough money for the pain that the teacher will have to go through? Do you think
25 that he or she will ever teach again after such an experience? The bets are on.

New Words:

_____

_____

_____

_____

_____

_____

_____

_____

_____

_____

Paparazzi

1　Twelve young photographers will have the chance to become famous in a show called "Paparazzi." How will they become famous? Their best shots will be all over the **tabloids** next fall. Their job will be to take the best pictures of superstars without them knowing it. They will secretly follow them around
5　to the grocery store, the restaurant and even the doctor's office. The show will be set in California, where it is easy for them to "**bump into**" a well-known actor or singer. Italian photographers will be the judges for this show and the rules are simple: the most embarrassing picture is the best picture.

　The winner will receive one million dollars and a feature article including their
10　photographs in many magazines. The runner-up will receive a fast car and a camera with a telephoto lens: tools he or she will need to excel in this trade.

　Paparazzi, a name you will not forget!

- After you read, look at the rules you highlighted. Were your inferences correct?

- In your opinion, which would be the best show? Which would you like to watch? Explain your answer, giving two reasons.

　_____

　_____

Work with Grammar

ARTICLES

- Underline all the articles in the text (*a*, *an* and *the*).

- Complete the rules and examples:

　You use *a* and *an*

　– in front of a _____ that you can count: *I'm reading* _____ *book.*

　– in front of a _____: *She is* _____ *actress. / He is* _____ *teacher.*

　– when giving the rate or pace of something: *They charge $250* _____ *day.*

　You use *the*

　– when talking about something we have already talked about:
　　Do you remember _____ *actor I told you about?*

　– when there is only one of it in the world: *You can watch the shows*
　　on _____ *Internet.*

　– in front of an important _____: _____ *Prime Minister of Canada*

　– in front of _____ of newspapers, buildings, hotels:
　　_____ *Gazette,* _____ *CN Tower,* _____ *Château Frontenac*

- Fill in the blank with the correct article.

　My mother is _____ comedian. She's performing in front of _____

　President of the United States. She make $1000 _____ day.

　See Grammar Workshop 3.1 on page 83 for more practice.

4 What makes good reality TV?

How do you choose the reality show you watch? Are you looking for huge fights? A bit of romance? Competition? A big prize?

A ● Read what makes a reality show interesting according to some teens.

● Rate each statement from 1 to 3.

❶ I really agree with that!   ❷ It's one of the reasons …   ❸ I totally disagree.

● Compare answers with a partner. Together, agree on what rating to give each statement.

Statement	My Rating	Our Rating
❶ For good reality TV, you need the people to be really different and have characters who don't get along. I like it when there are fights.		
❷ Reality shows are interesting to watch because you see what celebrities are like in real life.		
❸ Honesty and natural behaviour make good reality TV.		
❹ Competition is what makes it good TV. I like it when they are all competing for one thing and would do anything to get it. That makes it interesting.		
❺ If you want to win a show, you must be popular and nice with everyone.		
❻ The best shows are when people's dreams come true.		
❼ The best shows have famous people who criticize what the contestants do.		
❽ I like it when they show people who are really untalented.		

Smart Talk

I put …
Really?
Why did you put …?
I'm surprised …
I think it's best to …
I don't think it's important to …

B ● Decide on the best personality traits and characteristics of a reality TV contestant.

● Read these characteristics and add one of your own.

● Choose the five most important ones and rank them in order of importance.

● Compare answers with a partner.

○ calm   ○ good talker   ○ physically strong

○ creative   ○ likes company   ○ sense of humour

○ good leader   ○ musical   ○ sporty

○ good listener ○ physically attractive ○ _____

5 Listen to a candidate's experience.

Do you watch your favourite TV show and wish you could be a contestant? Listen to Mark Carnright, a contestant on an imaginary reality TV show, describe his experiences. The show was called "I'm Japanese Now." Mark had to pretend that he was Japanese when in fact he was a North-American **Caucasian**.

- Before you listen, look at the Smart Words and their definitions.

- Write a sentence using each word or expression.

Caucasian: _____

_____

contestant: _____

_____

awkward: _____

_____

take sides: _____

_____

worth the trouble: _____

_____

- Read the questions and write predictions for the answers. Remember to keep the title of the show in mind.

- After you listen, answer the questions and compare your predictions with the answers.

  1. How did Mark and the other contestants prepare for the reality TV show? Name at least three things.

  Prediction: _____

  _____

  _____

  Answer: _____

  _____

  _____

  2. How tall is Mark?

  Prediction: _____

  Answer: _____

  3. Why did Mark apply to this reality TV show?

  Prediction: _____

  Answer: _____

  _____

Smart
Words

Caucasian:
white-skinned

contestant: competes
in a competition

awkward:
uncomfortable or difficult

take sides: support
one person against
another person

worth the trouble:
interesting, enjoyable
or profitable

COMPANION **web+** You can try an
extra listening
activity using this text on
the Companion Website.

4. Why was Mark chosen for this TV show? What did Mark emphasize on his application to the show? Why do you think this helped him get on the show?

Prediction: _____

_____

_____

_____

Answer: _____

_____

_____

_____

_____

5. What do you think would be the hardest part for you about being on this show?

Prediction: _____

_____

Answer: _____

_____

_____

Here are other interview questions that were not asked.

- Read the questions and write an additional question.
- Sit with a partner. Pretend that one of you is the interviewer and one of you is Mark.
- If you are the interviewer, write your partner's answers. Then switch roles.

   1. Was it weird having cameras following you around all the time? Can you describe the experience?

   _____

   _____

   2. When you saw the show on air, what was it like?

   _____

   _____

   3. Do you have any advice for people going into reality TV?

   _____

   _____

   4. _____

   _____?

   _____

   _____

6 Have you got what it takes?

You want to be on TV but you can't act. Do you have the confidence to make it? Do you have a distinct personality? Read this text on how to get accepted onto a reality TV show and find out.

- Before you read, write what you think TV producers are looking for in new contestants.

  _____

- Read the questions after the text.

- While you read, take notes to help you answer the questions. Highlight or circle important information.

Have You Got What It Takes?

1 Do you want to be famous? Do you want to be on TV but can't act? No problem, just try out for a reality TV series. The producers of reality television are not looking for good actors, just lots of drama. If you've got a strong personality or you're quite manipulative, you too could be the star
5 of your own reality TV show. Here are a few tips to help you get started.

❶ If you know someone who works for the reality TV show you would like to be on, call that person first and see if she or he can help you get an audition. The important thing is to ask. Take a risk.

❷ Most reality TV shows require you to complete an **extensive** application
10 form and submit a video of yourself in action. They want to see what you look like on tape before they even meet you. Be yourself in the video and make sure the video is good enough quality that people can hear you on it. Look your best and put some thought into what you will say and how you will present yourself.

15 **❸** Take the time to read through the application form carefully before completing it. Don't leave any question unanswered. The people who make reality TV are actually looking for very specific personality types, and they are really interested in how you answer their questions. If you are looking to get married but don't believe in true love, they
20 want to know why! If you want to be on a show that will take you around the world but HATE to travel, you'd better explain your reason.

❹ Although these shows will never admit it, they are looking for stereotypical personalities who will create drama on screen. If you are loud, **obnoxious** and opinionated, if you are shy and sensitive, or if
25 you are confident and determined, they want to know all about that. Your answers should reflect your personality type. Watch the show you want to apply for and try to identify the personalities present. Who are you most like?

❺ After completing your application form, take the time to come up with
30 a good idea for your audition video. Really think about what your talents are and try to **feature** these. If you are a great singer, sing your heart out! If you are creative, let this shine in the way you present yourself on camera. What can you do that makes you unique and interesting?

Smart Words

extensive: complete
obnoxious: extremely unpleasant
feature: show

Notes:

_____
_____
_____
_____
_____
_____
_____
_____
_____
_____
_____
_____
_____

Notes:

_____

_____

_____

_____

_____

_____

_____

_____

_____

_____

▶

6 Take a chance and apply! The main thing you need to remember when
35   applying for any reality TV show is to let your true personality shine
through, good parts and bad parts. Be yourself and show the real you.

7 If you don't get a response from the producers of the television show
you applied to, don't get discouraged. There are new reality TV shows
out every season. Keep trying and make sure you apply to shows that
40   really interest you.

8 If you are really serious about becoming a contestant on a reality show,
check out the Web to find the closest reality TV schools. They do exist
and they will give you clear advice not only on how to get noticed when
applying but most importantly on what to do once the cameras are on.

45 **9** If you do get called in for an audition, be prepared. Remember, just
because you have an audition doesn't automatically mean that you
have been chosen for the show. Research the show you are auditioning
for carefully. Find out as much information about it as possible before
the audition and prepare yourself.

50 **10** If you do get called, scream "Hooray" and do your best! Go for it!

• **After you read, use your notes to answer these questions.**

  1. What is the easiest way to get on a reality TV show?

    _____

  2. What do reality TV shows usually require you to submit?

    _____

  3. What are shows looking for in the answers people give the application?

    _____

  4. What should the audition video feature?

    _____

  5. Think of a person you know who would be a great contestant for a reality
show. Explain why and in what type of show this person would have chances
of winning.

    _____

    _____

    _____

    _____

    _____

  6. Read these extra tips and put them in order of importance, according to you.
Share your list with a partner.

    _____

○ Be honest in your application form.

○ Apply even if you don't have the best physical features.

○ Know the show in case the producers ask you questions.

○ Emphasize your faults.

○ Don't be shy.

Work with Grammar

PRONOUNS AND POSSESSIVE ADJECTIVES

- Underline all the pronouns and possessive adjectives in the text.

- Complete the chart, the rules and the examples.

Pronouns				Adjectives
Subject	Object	Reflexive	Possessive	Possessive
I	me		mine	my
you	you	_____ / yourselves	yours	
he, she, it	_____, her, it	himself, herself, itself	hers, his	her, his, _____
we		ourselves		our
	them	themselves		

Most possessive pronouns take an *s* at the end. For example: *It is her____.*

To form reflexive pronouns, you add _____ (singular) or *selves* (plural) to the end of the possessive adjective.

Examples: *The dog hurt it_____. They watched them_____.*

- **Choose the right pronouns and possessive adjectives to replace the words in parentheses.**

   1. (Mike) told (Tania) not to watch the show.

   a) He / her   b) She / he   c) She / him

   2. That book (belongs to him).

   a) is his   b) is he   c) is him

   3. Charlie bought (a gift) for (Valérie).

   a) its / hers   b) it / her   c) itself / hers

   4. (My mom and my dad) gave (Jacob) books for (Maika's) birthday.

   a) They / him / her   b) They / he / hers   c) He / his / hers

   5. (Pat) made (complaints) about (his roomates).

   a) Him / them / theirs   b) He / it / themselves   c) He / them / them

See Grammar Workshop 3.2 on page 85 for more practice.

7 Write your script for your application to a reality TV show.

You have learned more about reality television. Now write a script for the video you will send to apply to become a reality TV contestant.

- **Refer to Writing Workshop 3 on page 91 for a model script.**

STEP 1 Prepare

- **What kind of show are you applying to?** _____
- **Think about what you want to say. Here are some ideas:**

1. Why do you want to be on the show? _____
_____

2. In what way will it change your life? _____
_____
_____

3. What do you like and not like? _____
_____

4. How you do deal with conflict? _____
_____
_____

5. What do people say of you? _____
_____
_____

6. What are your top two characteristics? _____
_____

- **Think of the emotions you want to get across. Will you be calm, excited …?**
_____

- **Where will you film yourself? At home? Outside?** _____
_____

- **Will you include other people in your script who can talk about your qualities?**
_____

- **Think of how you will bring your script to life. What you will do during the video? Will you sit? Stand? Dance? Sing? Scream and laugh? What will you wear?**
_____
_____
_____

STEP 2 Write

Write your script here. Include a description of the action.

_____
_____
_____
_____
_____
_____
_____
_____
_____
_____
_____
_____
_____
_____
_____
_____
_____
_____
_____
_____
_____
_____

STEP 3 Revise and Edit

- Reread your script. Did you answer all the questions in Step 1?
- Check spelling and grammar. Did you use articles, pronouns and possessive adjectives correctly?
- Ask a classmate to look at your script and comment.

STEP 4 Publish

- Learn your script and film yourself.
- Hand in your script and your video to your teacher.
- Watch your videos in class.
- Rate your video from 5 to 0: _____

  5 Excellent! The producers will choose me!   **0** They will never ever call me!

  Explain why you gave it that rating.

  _____
  _____

Name: _____ Group: _____ Date: _____

 8 # What are the best challenges?

Think of your favourite action reality TV shows and the challenges participants have to do in order to win. What are the best challenges?

- **Name two challenges that you have seen. Describe them briefly.**

  1. _____

  _____

  2. _____

  _____

- **Find three partners and form a team.**

- **Read the challenges below and vote on the following:**

  (A) The three that you could win

  (B) The three that you could never do

  (C) The three that are the most interesting to watch

A   B   C

○ ○ ○   **1.** Eat spiders

○ ○ ○   **2.** Go down a skyscraper with a harness

○ ○ ○   **3.** Jump off a bridge

○ ○ ○   **4.** Drive a car through a wall of fire

○ ○ ○   **5.** Put your head in a jar full of tarantulas

○ ○ ○   **6.** Have your body covered with bees

○ ○ ○   **7.** Swim with sharks

○ ○ ○   **8.** Take a very cold shower for five minutes

○ ○ ○   **9.** Eat ten chocolate bars

○ ○ ○   **10.** Drink pig's blood

○ ○ ○   **11.** Not sleep for forty-eight hours

○ ○ ○   **12.** Walk on broken glass

Smart Talk

I could never …
I could … for sure.
Number … is the most interesting, because …
Really?
I don't agree …
I saw it once and it was …

- **Compare answers with another team.**
- **Have a class vote for the most popular answers in A, B and C.**
- **Read the challenges again and try to put them into two different categories.**
- **Write the category titles and the numbers of the challenges in the chart.**

Category:	Category:
Challenges:	Challenges:

9 Learn reality TV basics.

Do you know if reality TV is really as popular as people say? How did this kind of TV start? Marc Cronin is a reality TV producer and gives his expert opinion.

- **Look at the Smart Words and circle the correct type of word.**

- **Before you watch the video, read the questions that the interviewer asks and guess the correct answer. Write a check mark.**

- **While you watch, check if your answers were right.**

1. What is "reality television"?

  ◯ It is the portrayal of real life. It is the closest thing to a documentary.

  ◯ It is a show that always portrays crazy people.

2. Is reality TV a new phenomenon?

  ◯ It only started in the last ten years.

  ◯ Reality television has been around literally since the birth of television.

3. What started the current wave of reality TV popularity?

  ◯ TV needed a new genre and these shows are inexpensive to produce.

  ◯ It started because viewers asked for it.

4. Why are reality shows so popular with audiences?

  ◯ Because viewers imagine what they would do if they were on the show.

  ◯ Because the shows are unpredictable and viewers like that.

5. How popular are reality shows?

  ◯ They dominate the other shows.

  ◯ They are the least-watched shows. Ratings are not that good, but as they are inexpensive to produce, they are still being shown.

6. How does reality TV differ from documentaries?

  ◯ Documentaries follow a journalistic standard.

  ◯ They are not different. Both of them show real-life situations.

- **After you watch, answer these questions as if you were a TV producer.**

1. How much do the amateur actors get paid for one show?

  _____

  _____

2. Are the shows scripted most of the time?

  _____

  _____

Smart Words

unscripted: without a script ((adjective) – verb)

plot: story (noun / verb)

sitcom: comedy show with a story (abbreviation of "situation comedy") (adverb / noun)

outcome: result (noun / adjective)

win-win: situation that benefits to everyone (verb / noun)

edit: cut and rearrange certain scenes (verb / adjective)

You can try an extra watching activity using this text on the Companion Website.

FINAL TASK

 10 Write a proposal for a new reality TV show.

Use everything you learned about reality TV to write a proposal for a new reality television show. It must be a reality show that promotes positive behaviour, such as helping others, rather than silly stunts!

STEP 1 Prepare

● **Brainstorm ideas for your proposal.**

Name of show: _____

Location of the show: _____

Basic idea or storyline for the show: _____
_____
_____
_____
_____

Type of contestants: _____
_____
_____
_____
_____

Challenges the contestants will perform: _____
_____
_____
_____
_____

What makes this show different from other reality shows: _____
_____
_____
_____
_____
_____

Prize for the winner: _____

STEP 2 Write

- Look at pages 68 and 69 to help you write your text.

_____
_____
_____
_____
_____
_____
_____
_____
_____
_____
_____
_____
_____
_____
_____
_____
_____
_____
_____
_____
_____
_____

STEP 3 Revise and Edit

- Reread your text. Does your text grab the reader's attention?
- Check spelling and grammar. Did you use articles, pronouns and possessive adjectives correctly?
- Ask a classmate to look at your work and comment.

Name of the person who reviewed my text: _____

Comments and suggestions: _____
_____
_____

STEP 4 Publish

- Read your text out loud to a partner or to the class.
- Have a class vote on who wrote the best proposal.

WRAP-UP

Try an extra activity using vocabulary from this unit on the Companion Website.

Test Your Smarts

● **Fill in the blanks in the sentences below with words from the unit.**

1. **R**_____ shows are very popular. TV producers are always looking for new **i**_____.

2. **C**_____ want to win. The **p**_____ is often money.

3. They want to become **f**_____. **M**_____ of viewers are hooked on reality TV.

4. These programs **f**_____ extrovert personalities. One guy on the show was really **o**_____!

5. The **a**_____ had a new girlfriend. His picture was in the **t**_____.

6. We had a **s**_____ teacher for a day. She disciplined the **l**_____ of the troublemakers.

Smart Expressions

● **Read the expressions below about reality TV.**

● **Choose the best definition for each one.**

I wanted to **escape from reality** by participating in that show.

Being on the show was a **reality check**. It was much harder than I thought.

1. To **escape from reality** means to

   a) get away from everyday life.   b) leave prison.   c) forget about your family.

2. A **reality check** means

   a) winning lots of money.   b) checking if everyone is okay.   c) seeing what is really happening or possible.

● **Write your own sentence using one of the above expressions.**

_____

GRAMMAR WORKSHOP 3.1

Articles

What do you know?

Do you know how to use definite and indefinite articles?

Example: There are **a** cow and **an** ostrich in **the** field.

- Circle the articles in the sentences below.
- Check your answers at the bottom of the page.

    Example: Sam has (a) television in his room so he can watch all
    (the) reality shows.

1. Sam wants to audition for a new reality TV show in the new year.

2. He has been taking a few classes to help him prepare for the audition.

3. Someone told him he has the looks and personality that producers look for in the business.

4. When he acted in the local theatre production, he received an honour from the mayor.

5. The next time you watch a reality TV show, maybe you will see him.

Score: _____/5

Rules

- Review the rules for definite and indefinite articles in the charts below.

Articles	
Definite articles (the)	Indefinite articles (a, an)
When do you use *the*?	**When do you use *a/an*?**
• When talking about something we have already talked about or something specific we already know about: Do you remember **the** reality TV show I told you about? • When there is only one: **the** Internet, **the** world • In front of an important title: **The** Prime Minister of Canada. • In front of the name of a newspaper, building, hotel: **the** *Gazette*, **the** CN tower, **the** Château Frontenac	• In front of a singular count noun (apple, dog, show): I read **a** review. She read **an** e-mail. • In front of a profession (dentist, teacher, actor): He is **a** reality TV show host. She is **an** artist on the show. • When giving the rate or pace of something: two miles **an** hour, fifty megabytes (MB) **a** second.

Answers: 1-a, the; 2-a, the; 3-the, the; 4-the, an, the; 5-the, a

Practice

Exercise 1

- Complete each sentence with the correct form of the indefinite article, **a** or **an**.

  Example: Jill received ___*a*___ call back from the TV show producer.

  1. Steve created _____ new reality TV show. I think it will be _____ extremely popular show.

  2. Will chose _____ girl from the show to take out on _____ interesting date.

  3. _____ element of surprise is important, especially in _____ reality TV show.

  4. I have never seen _____ reality TV show that is more than _____ hour long, unless it was _____ season opener or _____ grand finale episode.

  5. Some reality TV shows are _____ hoax, because you think that _____ event is happening naturally, but really it is _____ elaborate set-up.

Exercise 2

- Complete each sentence by adding a definite or an indefinite article where necessary.

  Example: ___*The*___ website is ___*an*___ excellent one and clearly lists all of ___*the*___ criteria for applying to ___*the*___ show.

  1. Kelly wants to complete _____ application process because _____ show has _____ really good reputation.

  2. _____ person who created _____ show is one of _____ best reality TV show producers in _____ world.

  3. _____ show isn't going to hire _____ girl without acting experience, so Kelly needs to find _____ good acting school to attend.

  4. _____ show could be _____ great way for Kelly to see if she has what it takes to become _____ actress.

  5. Kelly wants to make _____ great impression and show _____ producers she is _____ girl they are looking for.

Exercise 3

- Fill in the spaces with *a, an, the* or no article at all (*NA*).
- Write the name of each reality TV show in the space provided.

  > Faking It   Survivor   The Bachelor/Bachelorette
  > Project Runway   The Amazing Race   Master Chef

  Example: One of ___*the*___ best reality TV shows is set in ___*a*___ large American city, ___*NA*___ New York, and has ___*a*___ supermodel as ___*the*___ host.
  Show: ___*Project Runway*___

  1. If you like to travel, this is _____ reality TV show that takes _____ contestants on _____ journey around _____ world. Show: _____

2. On this _____ reality show, contestants cook _____ signature dish from _____ Michelin star chef's kitchen using only _____ ingredients they can taste in _____ sample dish. Show: _____

3. Maybe you will meet _____ love of your life and get married on _____ show like _____ one we're thinking of. Show: _____

4. On this _____ show, when Gordon Ramsay tried to train _____ contestant to be _____ top chef in just two weeks, it almost became _____ huge disaster when _____ contestant walked off _____ set during filming.
Show: _____

5. In _____ remote location, _____ contestants compete for _____ prizes and vote one another off _____ show until only one contestant remains.
Show: _____

GRAMMAR WORKSHOP 3.2

Pronouns and Possessive Adjectives

What do you know?

Do you know how to use pronouns and possessive adjectives?

Example: Did **you** see **him** take **his** turn before **her**?

● Circle the correct answer to replace the words in parentheses.

● Check your answers at the bottom of the page.

Example: (The TV host) encouraged (the contestant) to answer the question.

> a) himself / her   (b) he / her   c) it / them

1. On the reality TV show, (Susan) told (Robert) to go home.

> a) he / her   b) she / he   c) she / him

2. That DVD of *Survivor* episodes (belongs to me).

> a) is mine   b) is my   c) is yours

3. Even the producer (Bill) didn't think (Suzie) was the right person for the part.

> a) him / hers   b) himself / she   c) himself / hers

4. (Kris and Tim) gave (Joan) a black eye on (Joan's) birthday episode.

> a) they / her / her   b) they / she / hers   c) he / her / hers

5. (Carol) gave gifts to (her friends), but (her friends) still voted (Carol) off the show.

> a) him / them / their / he   b) he / it / thems / him   c) she / them / they / her

Score: _____/5

Answers: 1-c; 2-a; 3-b; 4-a; 5-c

Rules

- Review the rules for using pronouns and possessive adjectives in the charts below.

Pronouns

- Pronouns replace nouns.

Joan wears **dresses** in every episode. ⟶ **She** wears **them** in every episode.

   ↕   ↕   ↕   ↕

subject   object   subject   object

- Reflexive pronouns refer to the subject of the sentence.

Joan wears the dresses to please **herself**.

   ↕   ↕

subject   reflexive pronoun

Subject pronouns	Object pronouns	Reflexive pronouns
I	me	myself
you	you	yourself
he, she, it	him, her, it	himself, herself, itself
we	us	ourselves
you	you	yourselves
they	them	themselves
She played with her jewels on the set.	She played with **them** on the set.	Later she sold them **herself** without telling anyone.

Possessive adjectives and pronouns

- Use possessive adjectives and pronouns to show ownership.

Joan sometimes gets **her** jewellery from **our** TV producer.

Possessive adjectives	Examples	Possessive pronouns	Examples
my	This is **my** ring.	mine	This ring is **mine**.
your	That is **your** watch.	yours	That watch is **yours**.
her, his, its	That is **her** necklace. The TV producer often sleeps in **his** chair.	hers, his	That necklace is **hers**. This chair is **his**.
our	We looked for **our** studio.	ours	This studio is **ours**.
your	We found **your** bracelets.	yours	These bracelets are **yours**.
their	They slept in **their** clothes.	theirs	Those clothes are **theirs**.

Practice

Exercise 1

- Complete each sentence with the correct subject and object pronouns.

  Example: (Zander) ___He___ wants to be on a reality TV show.

  1. (Zander) _____ wants (Maria) _____ to stop calling him so much.

  2. (Maria) _____ thinks (Zander) _____ isn't being realistic about getting on a show.

  3. (I) _____ went to an audition with (my sister) _____ rather than go to (the audition) _____ alone.

  4. Every Saturday, (my father) _____ wants (my mother) _____ to watch an episode of reality TV with him, but (my mom) _____ says she hates (the episodes) _____ all.

  5. (Jon and Zoe) _____ avoid (reality TV shows) _____ by not watching TV.

Exercise 2

- Complete each sentence with the correct reflexive pronoun.

  Example: Jim wrote the script ___himself___.

  1. Valerie came up with the idea for the surprise gift _____.

  2. They took a photo to remind _____ of their time on the island.

  3. Andrew cleaned the house _____, but Craig said they did it together.

  4. I wrote the script for that reality TV show _____.

  5. On the show, Phil told Sarah that a gift is always nicer if you make it _____, but then he went and bought her one.

Exercise 3

- Underline all the pronouns and possessive adjectives.

- Identify what kind of pronouns and adjectives they are:
  SP for subject pronouns, OP for object pronouns, RP for reflexive pronouns, PP for possessive pronouns and PA for possessive adjectives.

  > Steven and I ___SP___ always watch reality TV with our ___PA___ friends. Last year, we _____ got together every week to watch *The Amazing Race*. I _____ found it _____ difficult to watch with so many people in my _____ house. It _____ was not that they _____ were loud, but they _____ all thought their _____ guesses were right when I _____ knew mine _____ were! I _____ myself _____ picked the winning team, although at the end of the day I _____ really don't care which team wins.

Try extra grammar exercises for pronouns and possessive adjectives on the Companion Website.

READING WORKSHOP 3

Inferencing

Inferencing is the ability to connect with a text or situation using your own thoughts, experiences and ideas. This connection helps you to make a better guess at what may really be happening.

We make inferences every day.

- **Write what you would think, or infer, in each situation.**

   1. Your mother is whispering on the telephone and quickly hangs up when you walk into the room.

   _____

   _____

   2. Your best friend turns red and can't speak in front of a certain girl in his class.

   _____

   _____

When you read a text, you infer in the same way. You are making an inference whenever you say things like these:

– *I realize that …*
– *Based on … I predict that …*
– *I can draw these conclusions …*
– *Based on this evidence, I think …*

Before You Read

- **Make inferences about what you are going to read by looking at the title, subtitles and other internal and external features of the text on page 89.**

- **Complete this sentence.**

   Based on what I can see in the text, I predict that the text will discuss

   _____

   _____.

While You Read

- **Highlight important information and ideas in the text.**

- **Complete the chart on page 89 with at least three important ideas from the text and three of your responses.**

I read that …	I think that …
Example: *Girls who regularly watch reality television accept and expect more drama and hostility from other girls in their everyday lives.*	*This is true because people imitate what they see on television.*

Girl Scouts: Reality TV causes "mean girl" effect

by Sandra Ecklund

1 **CHARLESTON, S.C. (WCIV)** — According to a national **survey** released by the Girl Scout Research Institute, girls who regularly watch reality television accept and expect more drama and hostility from other girls in their everyday lives.

5 In a survey of more than 1,100 tween and teen girls, a vast majority of them say that reality shows like *Jersey Shore* and *The Hills* are "mainly real and unscripted." They also come to expect the kind of reality portrayed in these shows including all of the aggression, bullying and the importance of physical appearances.

10 Loretta Graham, chief executive officer of the Girl Scouts of Eastern South Carolina, says the findings of the study clearly document the "Mean Girl" effect.

"The effect of media on girls shows the need for Girl Scouts," Graham said, "Girls need a place and avenue to address issues they have where they feel
15 safe and understood. Girl Scouts teaches them the skills to process situations and deal with them in an appropriate manner while supporting them in their goals."

You're so vain

While vanity has always been part of growing up into a young woman,
20 today's programming has become much more over-sexualized than in years past, according to the survey.

Results show 72 percent of regular reality show watchers said they spend a lot of time on how they look as opposed to only 42 percent of non-viewers. A higher percentage of reality show viewers also agreed, "They would rather
25 be recognized for their outer beauty than their inner beauty."

Smart **Words**

survey: questionnaire
vain: self-admiring

Smart Words

outgoing: friendly, sociable

But what about the good things about reality TV?

Believe it or not, there was an upside to the study. More than half (68 percent) of the respondents agreed that reality shows "make me think I can achieve anything in life." Also, the girls who say they watch reality
30 shows regularly saw themselves as more confident, stronger leaders and more **outgoing** than non-viewers saw themselves. That's one result the Girl Scouts, and Graham, can stand behind.

"Within Girl Scout programming, girls learn to love who they are and their talents ... develop a strong sense of self, develop positive values, gain practical
35 life skills, seek challenges in the world and develop critical thinking."

Source: Sandra Ecklund, "Girl Scouts: Reality TV causes 'Mean Girl' effect," *ABC News 4 Charleston*, Oct. 21, 2011, updated Nov. 16, 2011. Web. Feb. 12, 2012.

After You Read

- Write check marks for two or more inferences you can make from the above text.

  ◯ Girls live boring lives without reality TV.

  ◯ Reality TV encourages girls to think more about their physical appearance than their personality.

  ◯ Girls know that reality TV isn't real and don't allow it to influence their lives.

  ◯ Reality TV makes people more confident, so it's not all bad.

  ◯ Loretta Graham would like more girls to become Girl Scouts.

- Use the inferences you identified above to write a short paragraph. Answer the question: Is reality TV a good or bad influence? Explain why.

  _____

  _____

  _____

  _____

  _____

WRITING WORKSHOP 3

Scripts

A script is the written dialogue used for movies, TV shows and plays. It contains not only the words the actors say but also their actions and their facial expressions. Film scripts are also called screenplays.

- Read the script below. Notice that official scripts are always typed in 12 pt Courier font.

- Write the following elements of a script in the correct places: scene number character, dialogue, action, place (where the action takes place) and time.

scene number

1. INSIDE A MOVING CAR.
   DAYTIME.

   Two teenage girls talk in a car. Isabella
   is driving the car. She seems nervous.

                    ISABELLA
                 (looking worried)

        I have something to tell you.

                      ROSE
                (sounding surprised)

        You're scaring me. Tell me what?

                    ISABELLA
        I don't know how to tell you.

                      ROSE
                  (very worried)

            Come on. Just tell me.

                    ISABELLA
   I saw you last week when you looked through my
            bag and stole some money.

                      ROSE
                (starting to cry)

   Isabella! I would never do anything like that!
    I was looking in your bag to find a brush.

                    ISABELLA
   (staring at her friend but not saying anything)

                   You liar!

                      ROSE

Information about the scene, starts on the left, not centred

Character's name, always capitalized and centred

Didascalia tells the actor what should be done and how. Written in parentheses right below the character's name.

Dialogue—always centred

```
                (still crying)
            You have to believe me!

                   ISABELLA
    (still staring at her friend and not looking
                 at the road)

                    ROSE
                 (screaming)

             Isabella! A car …

      Sound of car that crashes.
```

Now, let's take a look at some of the internal features of a script.

Characters

- Identify the characters in the script.

  _____

- Describe the characters. What are they like?

  _____

  _____

  _____

Script descriptions can include age, physical characteristics and specific actions, such as tics and facial expressions.

Example: _Luca_

Handsome blond teenager, brown eyes, freckled face. Sixteen years old. Chews gum.

- Describe yourself in simple words as though _you_ were a character in a script. Include your age and any physical characteristics.

  _____

  _____

- Describe a friend or an imagined enemy in the same way.

  _____

  _____

  _____

  _____

  _____

Dialogue

A dialogue is a conversation between two or more people. Good dialogues include emotions.

- **Which of the dialogues is the best? Explain why.**

Dialogue 1

CHRISTOPHER
We should not say
anything.

ZACH
Hum?

CHRISTOPHER
You know!

ZACH
You promised me!

CHRISTOPHER
I know.

ZACH
Whatever.

Dialogue 2

CHRISTOPHER
(looking worried)
We should keep
this between us.

ZACH
(very angry)
Are you crazy? We
have to report
this to the police!

CHRISTOPHER
(on his knees)

Please Zach. If we go
to the police, they
will question us.

ZACH
(starting to cry)
We didn't do anything
wrong. I can't keep
this to myself.

_____

_____

Action

The action in a script is described on the left side of the page before, during or after a scene. It is written in short sentences in the present tense.

Here's an example of action in a script:

Charles walks down the stairs. He falls down.

- **Change the sentence below to show action in a script.**

Audrey was looking for her phone in her big purse, and then it fell on the floor.

_____

_____

Didascalia

The didascalia is written in parentheses right below the name of the character. It tells the actor what the character should do and how.

● **Choose the best didascalia.**

1. I think I'm going to bed now.

a) Elias smiles.   b) Elias cries.   c) Elias yawns.

2. I just saw a spider.

a) Cara walks.   b) Cara screams.   c) Cara speaks.

It's Your Turn

● **Write one scene of a script from reality TV on one of these topics or choose your own topic.**

1. Two contestants fighting over a prize

2. A contestant sharing a secret with his/her mother

3. Another topic from reality TV: _____

Script:

_____
_____
_____
_____
_____
_____
_____
_____
_____
_____
_____
_____
_____

Checklist

◯ Did you include the scene number, the place and the time of day?

◯ Did you include dialogue?

◯ Did you describe the characters?

◯ Did you describe the action?

◯ Did you include the didascalia?

What does beauty mean to you?

Why do all the people in magazines and in advertising look so beautiful?
Are they for real? Not always … What is beauty anyway? Let's find out.

- Look at the pictures of models on this page.
- Circle areas you think have been modified or altered.
- Take two minutes to write as many synonyms for the word *beautiful* as you can.
- Compare lists with a partner.

Beautiful: _____   _____

_____   _____

_____   _____

_____   _____

_____   _____

SMART START

1 Talk about what is attractive to you.

- Read the discussion questions and the Smart Talk below.
- Choose the Smart Talk phrases you will need and write words and ideas you will use.
- Take turns asking and answering the questions with a partner.

Partner 1

1. Do you consider muscular people to be more attractive? Why or why not?

2. What qualities should someone have to be attractive?

Words/Ideas:

_____
_____
_____
_____
_____
_____

Smart Talk

○ I believe this, because …

○ Another reason why …

○ Why do you say …?

Partner 2

1. Whose opinion do you agree with more in the cartoon?

2. Do you think people appreciate you more for your physical traits or for your personality? Why?

Words/Ideas:

_____
_____
_____
_____
_____
_____

2 Read about skinny models.

Do you think that the models you see in magazines and on the runway are too skinny? Read this text to find out what happened at a fashion show in Europe.

- **Skim. Find the main ideas of the text.**
  - Read the first paragraph.
  - Then, read the first sentence in each paragraph.
  - Finally, read the last paragraph.

- **Use what you learned when skimming to answer these questions.**

  1. What is the problem?

  _____

  _____

  2. Where is this happening?

  _____

  3. Who says this is a problem?

  _____

  _____

  4. How do they decide who is too skinny?

  _____

Skinny Models Banned from Catwalk

MADRID, Spain—The world's first **ban** on overly thin models at a top-level fashion show in Madrid has caused **outrage** among modelling agencies.

Madrid's fashion week has turned away underweight models after protests that girls and young women were trying to copy their **rail-thin** looks and developing eating disorders.

Organizers say they want to project an image of beauty and health, rather than a **waif-like** or "heroin-chic" look.

But Cathy Gould, of New York's Elite modelling agency, said the fashion industry was being used as a **scapegoat** for illnesses like anorexia and bulimia.

"I think it's outrageous. I understand they want to set this tone of healthy, beautiful women, but what about discrimination against the model, and what about the freedom of the designer?" said Gould, Elite's North America director, adding that the move could harm careers of naturally "gazelle-like" models.

Madrid's regional government, which sponsors the show and imposed restrictions, said it did not blame designers and models for anorexia. It said the fashion industry had a responsibility to portray healthy body images.

"Fashion is a mirror and many teenagers imitate what they see on the catwalk," said regional official Concha Guerra.

The mayor of Milan, Italy, Letizia Moratti, told an Italian newspaper this week she would seek a similar ban for her city's show unless it could find a solution to "sick-looking" models.

Smart Words

ban: prohibition
outrage: great anger
rail-thin: extremely thin
waif-like: extremely pale and thin
scapegoat: someone who is blamed for the something that is not her or his fault

▶

▶ The Madrid show is using the body mass index or BMI—based on weight and height—to measure models. It has turned away 30 percent of women who took part in the previous event. Medics will be on hand at the September 18 to 22 show to check models.

"The restrictions could be quite a shock to the fashion world at the beginning, but I'm sure it's important as far as health is concerned," said Leonor Perez Pita, director of Madrid's show.

Source: "Skinny models banned from catwalk," Madrid, Spain, Reuters, September 13, 2006.

- **Answer these questions.**

   1. Do you think that skinny models and the fashion industry inspire diseases like anorexia and bulimia? Why or why not?

   _____

   _____

   2. Do you think that the "skinny model" ban should be extended to all fashion media? Why or why not?

   _____

   _____

Work with Grammar

COMPARATIVE AND SUPERLATIVE ADJECTIVES

- **Find and underline the adjectives in the text.**
- **Complete the chart.**

Adjective	Comparative	Superlative
1. *thin*	*thinner*	*the thinnest*
2 *healthy*	*healthier than*	*the healthiest*
3 *beautiful*	*more beautiful than*	*the most beautiful*
4		
5		

- **Fill in the spaces to complete the rules.**

   Comparative form: For one-syllable adjectives, add **er + than.**

   For two- or three-syllable adjectives, add **more + than**.

   Superlative form: For one-syllable adjectives, add **the + est**.

   For two- or three-syllable adjectives, _____.

- **Fill in the blanks with the correct form of the adjective.**

   1. Most models are _____ (skinny) normal people.

   2. _____ (attractive) people in the world are healthy people.

See Grammar Workshop 4.1 on page 111 for more practice.

Name: _____ Group: _____ Date: _____

 **3** Look at an alternative ad.

Many companies are changing their ads to show "real" people. Here is an example of an advertisement for teens.

- **Look at the ad carefully. Do you think that this picture was modified?**

Your Beauty, Your Way

Dermatologists know that makeup can **harbour** acne-causing bacteria. That moisturizers can **clog** your pores, causing nasty blackheads and whiteheads. That many cosmetics contain allergens like lanolin (grease secreted by sheep) and carmine (made from crushed beetles) that can give you rashy, blotchy skin.

So why does the beauty industry insist that you need their products to be pretty? Do they make more money when you're happy and confident? Or when you're **plagued** by "imperfections" that they just happen to be able to "fix"?

Luckily, it's easy to take care of your skin without buying into the game. Wash it gently.

Get plenty of sleep. Drink water. Exercise. Eat lots of fruits and vegetables. Don't overdo it in the sun. Easy, inexpensive and natural.

Why let the beauty industry tell you how to feel about yourself?

It's your beauty.
Do it your way.

Smart **Words**

harbour: contain
clog: block
plagued: irritated

_____
AdBusters Media Foundation, Vancouver, British Columbia, Canada

Express Yourself Plus • Unit 4

99

A ● **Skim the ad on page 99 to find the main ideas.**

Main Ideas ***What?*** What is the ad trying to sell? _____

Who? Who is the "model"? _____

Why? What is the purpose of the ad? Circle one or more answers.

  a) To express feelings b) To inform you c) To influence you

● **Answer these questions.**

1. What can makeup and cosmetics do to your skin?

_____

_____

2. Does the beauty industry make more money when you feel happy or when you are feeling insecure? Explain your answer.

_____

_____

_____

3. What are some of the simple (and free) things you can do to take care of your skin? (Find at least five).

_____

_____

_____

4. What did you learn that was new or interesting?

_____

_____

5. Do you think that it is possible to change the advertising industry? Why or why not?

_____

_____

_____

B ● **Find each of these words in the text of the ad and underline it.**

● **Match each word to its synonym.**

1. nasty   ○   a) exaggerate

2. blotchy   ○   b) horrible

3. insist   ○   c) repair

4. fix   ○   d) spotted

5. overdo   ○   e) argue

Name: _____ Group: _____ Date: _____

4 Learn about "real beauty" in advertising.

Listen to a text that explains how "real beauty" is possible—even in advertising.

- Before you listen, read all the sentences carefully.
- While you listen, put the sentences in order.

A New Trend in Advertising

○ An Australian magazine just started using models who look like real women on its cover, and it has received thousands of letters from grateful readers.

○ A few years ago, it was unimaginable to dream about having your face on a billboard if you didn't have long legs or the perfect face. […] Looking for new concepts, in which the stars aren't top models but people just like you, is a new idea for advertisers.

(1) The people we see in the media represent only a small percentage of the different types of people who live in the real world, and this is a problem.

○ Anybody can become a poster star nowadays; anybody can become famous if they get the chance to be on TV; anybody can become a celebrity in only a few weeks. Whatever they look like—short-haired, long-haired, young, old, dark, pale—all looks are welcomed.

○ This starts early on. Even primary school children feel the need to wear the latest fashions, and girls as young as six are already worried about being fat or not pretty enough.

○ Consumers like the change they are seeing. Advertising now has a new different future.

○ When we see the same type of people every time we turn on the TV or open a magazine, it can make us feel dissatisfied with the way we look.

○ Consumers are now realizing how difficult it is to live with such high beauty standards.

- After you listen, read the following words from the text you just heard and their definitions.
- Circle the correct answer.

1. "An Australian magazine … received thousands of letters from **grateful** readers."
   If you are **grateful**, you
   a) appreciate what someone has done.   b) are angry.

2. "… having your face on a **billboard**."
   If your face is on a **billboard**, you can see it
   a) when you read a magazine.   b) when you drive a car.

3. "… it can make us feel **dissatisfied** with the way we look."
   If you are **dissatisfied**, you
   a) appreciate yourself.   b) don't feel good about yourself.

4. "… different types of people … live in **the real world**."
   Someone who **lives in the real world** is
   a) an ordinary person.   b) a celebrity.

5. "… girls as young as six are already **worried**."
   Someone who is **worried**
   a) feels contentment.   b) feels stress.

COMPANION web+ You can try an extra listening activity using this text on the Companion Website.

5 What is beautiful to you?

Now it is your turn to decide what makes a person beautiful. Is it the person's physique, personality or a combination of both traits? Write a paragraph explaining what you think makes someone beautiful.

STEP 1 Prepare

- Write ideas about what you think makes a person attractive. Think of someone you know to help you.

- Include important words and adjectives you will use.

_____
_____
_____
_____
_____

STEP 2 Write

Write the topic sentence. Example: *People can be beautiful in different ways.*
_____
_____

Give some facts or details.

One way a person can be beautiful is _____
_____

Explain your statement: *For example,* _____
_____

Give some facts or details.

People who believe that real beauty is _____
are wrong because _____

Explain your statement: *For example,* _____
_____

Summarize your ideas (closing sentence).

In the end, a person who is really beautiful is _____
_____

STEP 3 Revise and Edit

- Did you clearly define what makes a person beautiful?

- Check spelling and grammar. Did you use comparative and superlative adjectives correctly?

- Ask a classmate to look at your work and comment.

STEP 4 Publish

- Write the final version of your paragraph on a separate piece of paper.

6 Are tattoos beautiful?

One fashion trend is very controversial: tattoos. Are tattoos beautiful? How many people in your class have tattoos? If you have a tattoo, does it make you feel more attractive? Is a tattoo a work of art?

What do you think of the person in the picture? Is she beautiful? Why or why not?

- **Answer these questions individually and then share your answers with a partner.**

- **Take turns asking and answering the questions. Use the Smart Talk to help you.**

1. Do you like the way the person in the photo looks? Why or why not?

_____

_____

2. Would you like your parents to look like this? Why or why not?

_____

_____

3. Do you agree that tattoos are ugly? Why or why not?

_____

_____

4. Do you agree that it should be illegal for people under eighteen to get a tattoo? Why or why not?

_____

_____

5. Do you think that having tattoos affects the kind of jobs you can do? Why or why not?

_____

_____

Smart
Talk

○ I think that …, because …

○ For example, …

○ The person in the photo is …

7 Watch a video about tattoos.

The word *tattoo* comes from the Tahitian word *tatau*, meaning "to mark." In this activity, you will watch a video explaining why people get tattoos and why people want to remove them. You will learn about the history of tattoos and why the tattoo culture in Borneo is disappearing.

You can try an extra watching activity using this text on the Companion Website.

• **Before you watch the video, write down what you know and what you would like to know about tattoos.**

What do you know about tattoos?	What would you like to know about tattoos?	What did you learn about tattoos?
They are permanent.	*How much do they cost?*	
❶	❶	❶
❷	❷	❷
❸	❸	❸

• **Watch the video twice. The second time you watch, write what you learned about tattoos.**

• **Answer these questions.**

1. What is one thing the film says you shouldn't do when you get a tattoo? Do you agree with this rule?

_____

_____

2. Do you have a different opinion about tattoos now that you have seen this video?

_____

_____

• **Look at the following words from the film. Match them to their definitions.**

1. laser ◯   a) declaration of personal values

2. interesting ◯   b) fascinating

3. pain ◯   c) giant reptile; mythical monster

4. artist ◯   d) intense beam of light

5. statement ◯   e) person who makes art

6. dragon ◯   f) physical suffering

8 Find out what your parents think about tattoos.

Do your parents think tattoos are beautiful? What would they say if you asked to get a tattoo?

- Read the text below and circle five words in the text that are new to you.

- Use a dictionary. Write the words and their definitions in the margin.

- Read the text again and match each of these topics to a paragraph.

(A) Getting tattoos is addictive.

(B) Most people think carefully before getting a tattoo.

(C) People are proud of their tattoos.

(D) What should parents do if their child wants a tattoo?

(E) Tattoos are meaningful.

(F) Tattoos can stop you from getting the job you want.

(G) Tattoos reflect your personal history.

New Words:

_____

_____

_____

_____

_____

_____

_____

_____

_____

_____

Permanent Pigment: Future Regrets

You're on the losing side of the tattoo battle

Here's one of the frustrating realities about the psychology of tattoos: future possibilities just don't enter into the equation.

1 No question, that's a parent's number one worry when it comes to tattoos: that their child will go out and get this permanent thing on her or his body with no thought to the future. Yet suddenly everybody has a tattoo —or at least it seems that way. So what should parents do?

Topic: (D)

2 To get some answers, I conducted a number of brief, informal, unscientific interviews. Basically, I went up to people—in a supermarket, an electronics store, a bookstore, a coffee shop—and asked them about their tattoos. With no exceptions, the people I spoke to were immediately and enthusiastically **forthcoming**. Here's what I found.

3 Most had multiple tattoos. The first person I spoke with, a man in his early twenties, had both arms covered. After he got his first one, he wanted another. If there was an open space it pleaded to him for a tattoo. "It's **addicting**," he said. ("Addicting" was a word I would hear a number of times.)

Topic: ( )

Smart **Words**

forthcoming: willing to give information

addicting: creating a desire for more

▶

▶

4 People's first tattoos in particular often had special personal meaning. One young woman said her first was her name on her back. Another's first was a sun on his **forearm** that he and his high-school band had agreed to get together—but he had backed out. When one of the band members died, he got his first tattoo at twenty as a memorial to his dead friend.

Topic: ◯

Smart Words

forearm: lower part of the arm between the hand and the elbow

get rid of: remove

5 People didn't necessarily regret their choices. One woman explained she would no longer choose what she had picked for her first tattoos, but she would not **get rid** of them because they were part of who she had been— her personal history drawn out on her skin.

Topic: ◯

6 I asked a group of young workers with bare arms why they chose not to have tattoos. Each one, in fact, did have a tattoo—they just weren't visible. When asked why, they answered in unison, "Jobs." They did not want to do something that would get in the way of their white-collar career plans.

Topic: ◯

7 So what does it all mean? First, tattoos are not going away any time soon. Second, you may not like the look of tattoos, but they are not all bad. There seems to be something self-affirming for people who choose to get tattoos—they're proud of them. They're a personal statement.

Topic: ◯

8 Also, getting a tattoo is not as impulsive an act as many think. People give much thought to their tattoos—what they mean, where they are going to put them, the possible consequences—though they do not always take the conservative route.

Topic: ◯

9 What does this mean for parents? Many teenagers under the age of eighteen want tattoos. But at this stage parents have real control. For one thing, at many places you have to be eighteen or have a parent's consent to get a tattoo. Also, they do hear your words. So tell them what you think. "At least wait until you are older. You may regret your choice now and it's something you will have to live with." Or: "As long as you live under this roof you will not get a tattoo." (Which is a bit of a bluff.)

10 Your kids will hear you. In fact, all except one of the people I talked to got their first tattoo after they were eighteen. Why not before? The most common answer: "Because my parents would kill me."

Source: Anthony E. Wolf, "Permanent Pigment: Future Regrets," *The Globe and Mail* website, October 16, 2007.

Name: _____ Group: _____ Date: _____

- **Answer these questions.**

   1. What word does the man with tattoos on both arms use to describe getting tattoos?

   _____

   2. Give two examples of tattoos people have that have special meanings.

   _____

   _____

   3. Why don't the young workers want to show their tattoos?

   _____

   _____

   4. How old do you have to be to get a tattoo in most places?

   _____

   5. What was the most common reason people gave that they did not get a tattoo before they were eighteen?

   _____

Work with Grammar

SIMPLE PAST TENSE

- Circle all the examples of the simple past tense or simple past tense negative you can find in the text. See page 199 for the Irregular Verbs List.

- Fill in the blanks to complete the rules about the past tense.

   1. For most verbs in the past tense, you add _____.

   2. Irregular verbs need to be memorized; for example: get → got

   go → _____   _____ → had   _____ → found

- Read this paragraph about someone who wants to get a tattoo.

- Change the verbs in bold from the simple present tense to the simple past tense.

> David: I really **want** _____ to get a tattoo. However, I **know** _____ my parents would not approve. When I **talk** _____ to them about getting a tattoo, they just **tell** _____ me I **am** _____ too young. My friend **says** _____ I should get one anyway. She **believes** _____ it **is** _____ the right thing to do. She **advises** _____ me to pretend I **am** _____ eighteen and go to the tattoo artist. I **don't know** _____ if this **is** _____ good advice. My parents **trust** _____ me.

See Grammar Workshop 4.2 on page 115 for more practice.

FINAL TASK

9 Create a poster ad promoting unusual beauty or a positive body image.

STEP 1 Prepare

- Choose the idea. What is beautiful: "large size," tattoos, piercings?

  _____
  _____

- Brainstorm: Who is the target audience for your product—men or women? How old are the people for whom you are advertising?

  _____
  _____
  _____

- Research: Look at billboards and magazines to find interesting and different ways to show the body.

- Write adjectives for your description. Try to use the comparative and superlative forms.

  _____
  _____
  _____
  _____
  _____

- Create the first draft of your poster.
- Write your text. Use ideas from the ad on page 99.
- Glue or draw pictures that show a positive and realistic body image.

STEP 2 Produce

- Is your poster attractive and interesting? Does it present a positive body image?

- Check spelling and grammar. Did you use comparative and superlative adjectives? Did you use the simple past tense where appropriate?

- Ask a classmate to look at your work and comment.

Name of the person who reviewed my text: _____

_____

Comments / suggestions: _____

_____

_____

STEP 3 Present

- Create a final version of your poster.

- Present it to the class.

- Use this chart to vote for the best ad.

	First Place	Second Place	Third Place
Which ad is the most effective?			
Which ad is the most realistic?			
Which ad is the most eye-catching?			

WRAP-UP

Test Your Smarts

- Fill in the blanks in this paragraph with words from the unit. Then, find these words in the word search puzzle. You can circle words horizontally, vertically, diagonally and backwards.

- Use the first fourteen leftover letters in the puzzle to discover the mystery word.

Do you want to be **b**_____? Start by being _____**lthy**—in your mind and in your body. Don't try to be like those _____**ght** models you can see on a **b**_____**d** or in a magazine. The most beautiful people in the world are not **w**_____**d** about their looks. They don't spend their time thinking about _____**chy** skin or how to **f**_____ their looks. They **in**_____ on staying healthy and happy.

Try an extra activity using vocabulary from this unit on the Companion Website.

T	B	S	E	L	F	F	C	B	O	U
S	N	L	F	I	I	D	I	E	N	B
I	N	C	O	X	E	L	V	D	Y	E
S	L	J	O	T	L	J	E	O	H	A
N	A	Q	G	B	C	R	T	C	T	U
I	T	C	O	V	W	H	K	O	L	T
V	L	A	G	E	E	W	Y	C	A	I
O	R	W	I	E	E	H	V	A	E	F
D	Q	G	B	H	P	N	B	T	H	U
Z	H	W	O	R	R	I	E	D	Y	L
T	D	U	P	J	F	O	O	B	Y	D

What is the only thing you need to be truly beautiful?

_ _ _ _ - _ _ _ _ _ _ _ _ _ _ _

Smart Expressions

In English we say, **"You can't judge a book by its cover."** This expression compares books with people.

- **What do you think it is saying about people? Circle the correct answer.**

a) You can't tell what someone's personality is like by their looks.

b) First impressions are important.

c) People judge you on what you look like.

d) Someone who looks good is usually a good person.

- **Do you believe this? Why or why not?** _____

The expression **Beauty is in the eye of the beholder** means that whether something is beautiful depends on who is looking at it.

- **Read the sentence again. What do you think the verb *to behold* means?**

a) to watch   b) to like   c) to think   d) to see

GRAMMAR WORKSHOP 4.1

Adjectives

What do you know?

Do you know how to create the equivalent, comparative and superlative forms of adjectives?

Example: She is a **beautiful** girl. She is **as beautiful as** her mother.
She is **more beautiful than** her sister. She is **the most beautiful** girl in the pageant.

- Complete the chart with the correct form of each adjective.
- Check your answers at the bottom of the page.

Simple	Equivalent	Comparative	Superlative
glamorous	as glamorous as		the most glamorous
	as plain as	plainer than	
good			the best
unsightly		more unsightly than	
	as few as		

Score: _____/10

Rules

- Review the rules about adjectives and their various forms in the chart below.

Adjectives

When do you use them?
- To describe nouns: Carl is a **nice** guy.
- To compare two or more nouns by using the equivalent (same), the comparative or the superlative forms.
- For the equivalent form, use *as … as*: **as** small **as**, **as** pale **as**, **as** big **as**.

Simple	Comparative	Superlative
For one-syllable adjectives that end in a consonant For one-syllable adjectives that end in consonant / vowel / consonant	add *–er + than*: small ⟶ small**er than** add a consonant + *–er*: big ⟶ bigg**er than** thin ⟶ thinn**er than**	add *the* + adjective + *–est*: **the** small**est** add *the* + adjective + consonant + *est*: **the** bigg**est**
For adjectives ending in *–e*	add *–r*: simple ⟶ simple**r than** wise ⟶ wise**r than**	add *the* + adjective + *st*: **the** simpl**est**

Simple	Comparative	Superlative
For one- or two-syllable adjectives ending in −y	change the y to i + −er + than: crazy ⟶ craz**ier than** busy ⟶ bus**ier than**	use the + adjective, then change the y to i + −est: **the** craz**iest** **the** bus**iest**
For two-syllable adjectives that do <u>not</u> end in −y	use more/less + adjective + than: extreme ⟶ **more** extreme **than** awesome ⟶ **less** awesome **than**	use the most / the least + adjective: **the most** extreme **the least** awesome
For adjectives with three or more syllables	use more/less + adjective + than: dangerous ⟶ **more** dangerous **than** spectacular ⟶ **less** spectacular **than**	use the most / the least + adjective: **the most** dangerous **the least** spectacular
Exceptions		
good	better than	the best
bad	worse than	the worst
little	less than	the least
few	fewer than	the fewest
far	farther / further than	the farthest / the furthest

Practice

COMPANION WEB+ Try extra grammar exercises for adjectives on the Companion Website.

Exercise 1

- **Underline each simple, comparative or superlative form of the adjective.**
- **Put each form in its correct category.**

  Example: Christine has <u>the most adorable</u> smile, but she doesn't smile often.

  1. When Sabrina wears her new clothes, she looks as fancy as a princess.

  2. Steve likes to wear the drabbest colours at school.

  3. Caroline is worse than Suzie when it comes to gossiping.

  4. Christian is as clever as anyone else in the class.

  5. Mrs. Philips is more energetic than most young teenagers, and she is eighty.

  6. Ken is the most mysterious man I have ever met.

  7. Kris was as gentle as he could be when he told Sarah how he felt about her.

  8. Persephone is a more faithful friend than Dominique.

Simple	Equivalent	Comparative	Superlative
			the most adorable

Exercise 2

- Write sentences for each adjective using the forms requested.

Example:

Simple: *Susie is careless.*

Equivalent: *Susie is as careless as John says she is.*

Comparative: *Susie is less careless than / more careless than her brother.*

Superlative: *Sam is the most careless person in the class.*

1. thoughtless

   Comparative: _____

   Equivalent: _____

2. grumpy

   Superlative: _____

   Simple: _____

3. gifted

   Superlative: _____

   Comparative: _____

4. obnoxious

   Equivalent: _____

   Simple: _____

5. good

   Comparative: _____

   Simple: _____

6. curvy

   Equivalent: _____

   Superlative: _____

Exercise 3

- Indicate whether the adjective in each sentence is correct or incorrect.
- Correct any incorrect sentences.

	Correct	Incorrect
Example: Jenny is the more nervous person in the world. *Correction: Jenny is the most nervous person in the world.*		✓
❶ Phil is as tall as Tiffany.		
❷ Cam is a handsomest guy.		

	Correct	Incorrect
3 Francine is sillier than Stephan, but Billy is the silliest person I have ever met.		
4 Mrs. Philips is more uptighter than Mr. Philips.		
5 Christine is as small as Tanja, but Peter is smaller than both of them.		
6 Jessica's style is modern and cool.		
7 My hair is greasiest today than yesterday.		
8 Justin is faster than Steve when getting ready to go out.		
9 James has the most sparklingest eyes.		
10 Tess has a more adorabler laugh than Mickey.		

Exercise 4

- Look around the class and note the appearance of your classmates.
- Describe their appearance using the appropriate forms of the adjectives you choose.

Example: *Sarah has beautiful long hair. Sarah's hair is longer than Tony's.*
Molly has the shortest hair in our class.

_____
_____
_____
_____
_____
_____
_____
_____
_____

Name: _____ Group: _____ Date: _____

GRAMMAR WORKSHOP 4.2

Simple Past Tense

What do you know?

Do you know how to use the simple past tense?

Example: He **thought** she **was** beautiful.

- Indicate whether the sentences are correct or incorrect.
- Underline each incorrect verb.
- Write it correctly.
- Check your answers at the bottom of the page.

	Correct	Incorrect
Example: Joannie <u>believe</u> she wasn't pretty enough. ***Correction: believed***		✓
❶ Jenny wore an outfit that made her eyes sparkle.		
❷ Jim worked out so much last week that he hurted his leg.		
❸ We went to the pool to swim, but it was closed.		
❹ Sophie putted on so much makeup that she lookt like a clown.		
❺ Tim didn't ate lunch at all this week because he aren't feeling well.		

Score: _____/5

Rules

- Review the rules for the simple past tense in the chart below.

Simple Past Tense
When do you use it?
● For actions that began and ended in the past

yesterday · · · now

Yesterday I ***talked*** to my teacher about my career.
(Action completed)

Affirmative	
Rule	Examples
Regular verbs: Add *-ed* to the base form of the verb.	I walk**ed** to school yesterday.
Irregular verbs vary. (See Irregular Verbs list on page 199 of the Reference Section.)	They **took** the train home yesterday. (take) We **ate** lunch hours ago. (eat) She **read** a book all afternoon. (read)

Key words: last night, yesterday, minutes ago, hours ago, today, last month, last year

Negative	
Rule	Examples
Add *did + not* (or the contraction *didn't*) + verb	I **did not walk** / **didn't walk** to school yesterday. I **did not take** / **didn't take** the train yesterday.

Question	
Rule	Examples
Add *did* + subject + verb?	**Did** you **walk** to school yesterday? **Did** you **take** the train yesterday?

COMPANION **Web** Try extra grammar **exercises** for the simple **past** tense on the Companion Website.

Practice

Exercise 1

● Circle all verbs in the simple past.

I (thought) that I (wanted) to date Cherry Stevens. We were in the same homeroom class in grade 9 and she always looked great. She had a slim body and long blond hair. She wore her hair down and she looked like an angel. She didn't wear too much makeup and her clothes were always in the latest fashion. She was one of the most popular girls in the school. When I finally asked her out and we went on a date, I was horrified to find that we had absolutely nothing to talk about. She didn't like any of the same movies that I did. She didn't watch any of the sports that I played at school because her friends didn't. She didn't like reading and she hardly ever listened to any of the bands I do. It was a total bust! She looked good, but we didn't connect at all. ·

Exercise 2

● Write the simple past tense of each verb.

● See the Irregular Verbs List on page 199 of the Reference Section.

Irregular Verbs			
Verb	Simple past	Verb	Simple past
❶ awake		⓫ run	
❷ become		⓬ see	
❸ bleed		⓭ shake	

Irregular Verbs			
Verb	Simple past	Verb	Simple past
4 deal		**14** steal	
5 feed		**15** stick	
6 find		**16** swear	
7 grow		**17** tell	
8 know		**18** think	
9 lend		**19** throw	
10 lie		**20** write	

Exercise 3

- Rewrite each verb in parentheses using the simple past.
- Rewrite each sentence in the negative (N) and question (Q) forms.

> **Example:** Terry (try) *tried* a new exercise routine to get in shape.
> N: *Terry did not try a new exercise routine to get in shape.*
> Q: *Did Terry try a new exercise routine to get in shape?*

1. Sarah (want) _____ to cut and dye her hair.

N: _____

Q: _____

2. Phil (wait) _____ until his birthday to get a tattoo.

N: _____

Q: _____

3. Sabrina (forget) _____ what a special person she is.

N: _____

Q: _____

4. Antoine (write) _____ an essay describing inner beauty.

N: _____

Q: _____

5. Bianca (grow up) _____ to be a confident woman.

N: _____

Q: _____

READING WORKSHOP ④

Skimming to Find the Main Idea

When you skim, read through the text quickly to get a general sense of what the main ideas are.

These are some effective ways to skim a text.

– Look at the pictures.

– Read the first paragraph.

– Read the last paragraph.

– Read the first sentence of each paragraph.

Before You Read

- Skim the personal essay below.

- Underline the correct answer.

  This text discusses

  1. someone who has struggled with cancer.

  2. someone who has struggled with making friends.

  3. someone who has struggled with anorexia and self-image.

  4. someone who has struggled with alcohol abuse.

- Think about what you already know about this issue. Do you know anyone who has this condition? What do you think is the cause?

  _____

  _____

  _____

While You Read

- Indicate the main idea in each section by underlining the correct answer.

Already Perfect
by Elisa Donovan

1

1 Everyone can identify with the need to fit in. Each one of us **struggles** with self-esteem and self-worth to some degree. I spent much of my time **striving** to achieve perfection in every aspect of my life. What I did not realize was that in my desperate need to be perfect, I sacrificed the very body and mind that allowed me to live.

5 **Example:**
Main idea: <u>Trying to be perfect can be deadly.</u> / Everyone struggles with self-esteem.

(2)

1 I was a happy kid with lots of friends and a supportive family. But **growing up** was really hard and even scary sometimes.

During my childhood, I was constantly involved in something that included an audience viewing my achievements or my **failures**. I was into acting by age
5 seven, and progressed to training for and competing in gymnastics, horseback riding and dance—all of which required major commitment, discipline and strength. My personality **thrived** on the high energy required to keep up. I wanted everyone's **praise** and acceptance, but I was my own toughest critic.

Main idea: The origin of her condition lay in being a happy kid with a supportive
10 family. / The origin for her condition lay in needing praise and being critical of herself.

(3)

1 After I graduated from high school and moved out on my own, my struggles with self-esteem and happiness increased. I began to put pressure on myself to succeed in the adult world. Meanwhile, I was feeling very inadequate and unsuccessful. I started to believe that my difficulties and what I perceived to be my "failures"
5 in life were caused by my weight. I had always been a thin-to-average sized person. Suddenly, I was convinced that I was overweight. In my mind, I was FAT!

Slowly, my inability to be "thin" began to torture me. I found myself involved in competition again. But this time, I was competing against myself. I began to control my food by trying to diet, but nothing seemed to work. My mind
10 became obsessed with beating my body at this game. I slowly cut back on what I ate each day. With every portion I didn't finish or meal I **skipped**, I told myself that I was succeeding, and in turn, I felt good about myself.

Main idea: She equated failure with being fat, and skipping meals was a sign of success. / She felt inadequate and unsuccessful.

(4)

1 Thus began a downward spiral of my becoming what is known as anorexic. The dictionary defines it as "suppressing or causing loss of appetite resulting in a state of anorexia." When taken to an extreme, anorexia can cause malnutrition and deprive the body of the important vitamins and minerals that it needs to be healthy.

5 **Main idea:** She started taking vitamins. / She became anorexic.

5

¹ In the beginning, I felt great – attractive, strong, successful, almost super-human. I could do something others couldn't: I could go without food. It made me feel special, and that I was better than everyone else. What I didn't see was that I was slowly killing myself.

People around me began to notice my weight loss. At first they weren't alarmed; maybe
⁵ some were even envious. But then the comments held a tone of concern. "You're losing too much weight." "Elisa, you're so thin." "You look sick." "You'll die if you keep this up." All their words only reassured me that I was on the right path, getting closer to "perfection."

Sadly, I made my physical appearance the top priority in my life, believing that it was the way to become successful and accepted. As an actress, I am constantly being judged by my
¹⁰ appearance. The camera automatically makes people appear heavier than they are. So I was getting mixed messages like, "Elisa, you are so skinny, but you look great on camera."

I cut back on my food more and more, until a typical day consisted of half a teaspoon of nonfat yogurt and coffee in the morning, and a cup of grapes at night. If I ate even a bite more than my allotted "**crumbs**" for the day, I hated myself and took laxatives to rid my
¹⁵ body of whatever I had eaten.

Main idea: Everyone thought she looked good thin. / Her physical appearance was her top priority and she started to look and act sick.

6

¹ It got to the point where I no longer went out with my friends. I couldn't—if I went to dinner, what would I eat? I avoided their phone calls. If they wanted to go to the movies or just hang out at home, I couldn't be there—what if food was around? I had to be home alone to eat my little cup of grapes. Otherwise, I thought I was failing.

⁵ Everything revolved around my strict schedule of eating. I was embarrassed to eat in front of anyone, believing that they would think I was gluttonous and ugly.

My poor nutrition began to cause me to lose sleep. I found it hard to concentrate on my work or to focus on anything for any length of time. I was pushing myself harder and harder at the gym, struggling to burn the calories that I hadn't even eaten. My
¹⁰ friends tried to help me but I denied that I had a problem. None of my clothes fit, and it was hard to buy any, since I had **shrunk** to smaller than a size zero!

Then one night, like so many nights before, I couldn't sleep, and my heart felt as though it might beat its way out of my chest. I tried to relax, but I couldn't.

The beating became so rapid and so strong that I could no longer breathe. The
¹⁵ combination of starving myself and taking pills to get rid of anything that I did eat caused me to nearly have a heart attack. I stood up, and immediately fell down. I was really scared, and I knew I needed help.

My roommate rushed me to the hospital, beginning the long road to my recovery. It took doctors, nurses, nutritionists, therapists, medications, food supplements …
²⁰ and most importantly, a new sense of what was really true about myself to get back on track with reality.

Main idea: Anorexia destroyed her social life and her physical health until she nearly died. / She started losing sleep.

⑦

1 **Recovering** from what I did to my body and reprogramming the way I think about myself has been a very slow and extremely painful process. I still struggle with the effects of anorexia every day. Although it has been a couple of years since that hospital visit, it is by no means over for me. I must be honest with myself and
5 stay committed to being healthy.

I had used my anorexia as a means of expression and control. I used it as my gauge for self-esteem and self-worth. It was my identity. Now I realize that the way to success lies in my heart, mind and soul, rather than in my physical appearance.

I now use my intelligence, my talents and acts of kindness to express myself. This is
10 true beauty, and it has nothing to do with the size of my body. With my experience of trying to be "perfect" on the outside, I had sacrificed who I was on the inside. What I know now is, we are—each and everyone of us—already perfect.

Main idea: True beauty has nothing to do with the size of your body—it's about who you are on the inside. / True beauty is about your physical appearance.

Source: Elisa Donovan, "Already Perfect," in *Chicken Soup for the Teenage Soul.* ed. by Jack Canfield, Mark Victor Hansen and Kimberly Kirberger (Deerfield Beach: Health Communications, Inc., 1998).

Smart Words

struggle: fight against or with something
strive: work very hard
grow up: become older
failure: not a success
thrive: flourish, succeed
praise: expression of admiration
skip: miss
crumb: very small amount
shrink: become smaller in size
recover: get better after an illness or injury

After You Read

● **Answer these questions:**

1. Elisa Donovan wanted to feel praised and accepted. Who judged her the most?

_____

2. What kind of childhood did she have?

_____
_____

3. How did she feel at the beginning when she started losing weight?

_____
_____

4. What did she eat on a typical day?

_____
_____

5. Why was she rushed to the hospital?

_____
_____

6. How does she express herself now?

_____
_____

WRITING WORKSHOP 4

Opinion Paragraph

An opinion is your chance to explain what you think about a subject. Your goal is to convince your audience that your opinion is valid.

An opinion paragraph is a body paragraph, which is one of the three main components of an essay (see Writing Workshop 2). The other two are the introduction and the conclusion.

Let's look at the features of an opinion paragraph about tattoos.

– Topic statement: This statement clearly expresses the main idea of the paragraph, that is, your opinion. It can be made up of more than one sentence.

- **Underline the better topic statement. Explain why it is better.**

1. Tattoos are a bad idea when you are young because you don't really know what they mean.

2. Tattoos are popular.

_____

_____

– Supporting statement 1: This is the place for the first argument that supports the topic sentence. Use facts and/or statistics. Minimize the use of "I."

- **Write your first argument.**

_____

_____

_____

– Supporting statement 2: Here is the place for a second argument that supports the topic statement. Use facts and/or statistics. Minimize the use of "I."

- **Underline the better argument. Explain why it is better.**

1. For example, this fifteen-year-old guy got a tattoo of a tribal sign, and now he thinks it is really silly and would like to get rid of it. He is thirty years old and the tribal sign does not mean anything to him anymore.

2. For example, this fifteen-year-old guy got a tattoo of a tribal sign and he still likes it ten years later.

_____

_____

_____

– Supporting statement 3: Here is the place for the strongest argument that supports the topic statement. Use facts and/or statistics. Minimize the use of "I."

- **Underline the best argument. Explain why it is the best.**

Tattoos are a bad idea because

1. they will look bad in twenty years.

2. they can cause health problems.

3. they are difficult to remove.

_____

_____

– Transition statement: Don't forget that if you are writing more than one body paragraph you will need to write a transition statement to link them. (See Writing Workshop 2.)

- **Underline the better transition sentence. Explain why it is better.**

1. Before making up your opinion on tattoos, you must be informed about what tattoos mean for a special tribe in Africa.

2. I believe that tattoos look good.

_____

_____

– Concluding statement: Place this sentence at the end of the paragraph and summarize the arguments strongly but briefly. It should leave the reader convinced that you have a valid point of view.

- **Underline the better concluding sentence. Explain why it is better.**

1. Tattoos are a bad idea because I believe so and so do most of my friends.

2. You should think twice before you get a tattoo, whether because of your age, because you don't understand their meaning or because they are difficult to remove.

_____

_____

Let's look at a model opinion paragraph.

- **Read the paragraph.**
- **Highlight the topic statement.**
- **Underline the three supporting statements.**
- **Double-underline the concluding statement.**

Plastic surgery should be avoided for many reasons. First, surgery always has risks and people who go under the knife face medical dangers such as skin discoloration, visible scars and even more serious consequences. Many women have removed their breast implants after they began having health problems. Another important reason is that plastic surgeons charge a lot of money. Patients spend weeks in private hospital bedrooms and their bills can easily go up to $20,000 for a simple procedure. But most of all, plastic surgery is an enemy of self-confidence. Many women who get cosmetic surgery obsess with their looks and are never happy. We do not support the idea of living in a world where everyone looks like Barbie and Ken.

It's Your Turn

- Write your own opinion paragraph beginning with one of the topic statements below or your own choice.

- Use the simple past tense and as many comparative and superlative adjectives as possible.

   1. Muscular men are more successful with women.

   2. Skinny models should not be hired.

   3. Another topic statement: _____

   _____

- Write three supporting statements that support your topic statement.

_____
_____
_____
_____
_____
_____

- Write a concluding statement.

_____
_____
_____

Checklist

◯ Did you stick to your opinion?   ◯ Did you use statistics?

◯ Did you use facts?   ◯ Did you minimize the use of "I"?

How can a project change the world?

In this unit, you will discover how we all have a responsibility to become involved if we desire to see real change happen.

Imagine that you are a professional photographer and you took this picture. Explain what is happening in the picture and the story behind it.

- **Use at least five of these words to describe the picture.**

> boys   donations   help   more   road   school
> change   future   money   Pakistan   United Nations

_____

_____

_____

_____

SMART START

1 Find new ideas for change.

Start small. What small things can you do to change your world? Do you try to take public transportation or ride your bike to get around instead of going by car, for example? Do you take short showers to use less water?

● **Write three more ideas. Think of what you or your parents do.**

   1. _____

   2. _____

   3. _____

● **Read the list of ideas in the chart below.**

● **For each idea, write who could do this and how this action can change the world.**

   Who? individuals, businesses, communities, governments

   How? reduce pollution, reduce energy use, help people in need

● **Circle three ideas that you would like to try.**

● **Compare answers with a partner. Use the Smart Talk to help you.**

I think I could …
I'm not sure about …
I put …
I always …

Ideas	Who?	How?
1. Buy biodegradable cleaning products	*Individuals*	*Reduce pollution*
2. Dry your clothes outside instead of in a dryer		
3. Learn another language		
4. Share a car		
5. Use less air conditioning		
6. Donate old laptops and cellphones to charity		
7. Design houses to utilize natural light		
8. Educate people around the world		
9. Provide free medication to people who can't afford it		
10. Travel the world by volunteering		

2 # Learn about extraordinary people.

These extraordinary people have had a special impact on the world.

- **Look at the pictures of these people and write a check mark beside the ones you are familiar with.**

- **Read each biography and underline a special thing this person has done.**

- **Circle all the words that are similar in French. See the examples in the first paragraph.**

- **Compare words with a partner.**

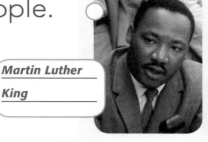

Martin Luther _____

King _____

1. He was an (American) (minister) in the (Baptist) church in the 1950s and 1960s. At that time in the United States, there was a (system) of (racial) segregation: blacks and whites used separate schools, (medical) facilities and (public) (transportation). His most influential speech, "I Have a Dream," (inspired) people to protest against (segregation).

2. He is a world leader in sustainable ecology and Canada's best-known environmental activist. This doctor examines how changes in science and technology affect our lives and the world around us. He has a TV program and criticizes governments for their lack of action on global warming.

3. He is a Canadian senator, humanitarian, author and retired general. He is best known for his involvement in the United Nations peacekeeping force in Rwanda in 1993 and 1994. He tried to stop the Hutus from slaughtering the Tutsis. He wrote a bestselling book that was subsequently made into a movie.

4. She won the Nobel Prize in 2003 and is the first female judge in her country. She works to promote the rights of women, children and refugees in Iran. She is the founder and leader of the association Support Children's Rights in Iran.

5. She is best known for her efforts to protect the endangered chimpanzee populations in Africa. She studied chimpanzees in Gombe Stream National Park in Tanzania, Africa for forty-five years. Now she travels all year, speaking about the threats facing chimpanzees and about other environmental crises.

- **Match each biography to the correct name. Write the number in the circle.**

  ( ) David Suzuki   (1) Martin Luther King   ( ) Shirin Ebadi

  ( ) Jane Goodall   ( ) Roméo Dallaire

- **Write the name of each person underneath her or his picture.**

You can try an extra watching activity using this text on the Companion Website.

3 Watch a video on what humanitarian workers do.

There are thousands of people around the world whose mission is to help others. They are humanitarian workers. You will watch two short videos, one on what humanitarian workers do and one about Marco Dormino, who talks about working with a family in Haiti.

Smart Words

wage: fight
disease: sickness, illness
shelter: house
hunger: insufficient food

A World Humanitarian Day Project–Humanitarian Workers

● Before you watch the first video, look at the Smart Words.

● Complete each sentence with a Smart Word.

1. Our _____ was a small tent.

2. In Africa, a lot of _____ could be avoided with vaccines.

3. We will _____ a campaign against poverty.

4. Children have no food; they are dying of _____ .

● Watch the video a first time.

1. What do you notice? What do you find beautiful?

_____

_____

_____

● Watch the video a second time.

2. Name ten countries involved.

_____

_____

● Watch the video a third time.

3. Name three things workers are doing to change the world. Write only the actions.

Work in every country, _____

_____

B World Humanitarian Day Project–Marco Dormino

● Watch the second video twice and answer these questions with complete sentences.

1. What is Marco's occupation?

_____

2. Why did he notice the little boy?

_____

3. What is different about the little boy?

_____

4. What did Marco do to help the family?

_____

5. Why does the family need a bike?

_____

_____

6. What job can the boy's father now do with the bike?

_____

7. What could you do to help people in Haiti?

_____

_____

8. Would you be interested in becoming a humanitarian worker? Why or why not?

_____

_____

4 Pitch your idea to the United Nations.

Imagine that you have thirty seconds to pitch an idea for changing the world to the United Nations Secretary-General. What would you say? We want to hear your ideas!

- **Think of what you just saw in the video.**

- **In what field would you like to make a change? Education? Health? Nutrition? Art? Another field?**

_____

- **Write your pitch. Make sure that you think of strong words to touch the United Nations Secretary-General.**

> *Dear Secretary-General, please listen. If I could change the world, I would ...*
> _____
> _____
> _____
> _____
> _____
> _____

- Read your pitch in front of the class.
- Compare the ideas presented and decide on the best one.

5 Read about Frédérique Vallières's initiative.

Frédérique Vallières, a young woman from Québec, co-founded the non-profit organization Reach Out to Humanity (ROTH), based on the principle that every human being has the right to proper health care, education, nutrition and shelter. The organization has worked on many projects, raising money to allow children to go to school, installing water pipes, building houses, providing prescription glasses and building a maternity ward.

- Read the interview below to find out more about Frédérique Vallières.

- Write three words you don't know in the margin and look up their definitions in a dictionary.

New Words

_____

_____

_____

_____

_____

_____

_____

Interview with Frédérique Vallières

1 **Frédérique, you look so young to have accomplished so much. How old are you?**

I am twenty-six years old.

How did you come up with the idea of starting ROTH?

5 ROTH came about after my first trip to Africa in 2006. My friends and I saw many children suffering from extreme poverty—children eating out of garbage cans, children walking around without shoes, children whose parents <u>couldn't</u> **afford** to send them to school. My friends and I wanted to change this, so we decided to form our own group to
10 make a difference. The goal is to be able to represent ROTH all over the globe. Over the last five years ROTH has grown into a network of over 100 volunteers, each of whom gives their time for various tasks both in Canada and in Africa. We have no paid employees, so we very much rely on people giving us their time and expertise.

15 **Why did you want to go to Kenya?**

After I graduated from university, I was ready to do some travelling. I always wanted to go to Africa, and I'd heard so many great things about Kenya. The people are wonderful, there are great sights to see, with many animals around, and most importantly, it is a safe place to travel to. Since
20 my first trip to Kenya, I have had the opportunity to travel to many places in Africa, including Tanzania, Uganda, Mauritania, South Africa, Senegal and Sierra Leone.

Would you say that your living conditions in Kenya are dangerous?

25 I wouldn't necessarily say that they are dangerous, but you have to be **aware** of your **surroundings**. We come from what others perceive to be a very wealthy nation—which we are—and when you are travelling in places where you automatically come off as a **foreigner,** you have to be careful where you go and at what time. You have to be smart and respectful of
30 other cultures when you travel.

▶

▶

Which obstacles were in your way, and how did you overcome them?

The biggest obstacles were finding some of the resources in Kenya that are so readily available in Canada. For the most part, we were able to find
35 everything, but sometimes we had to order them from Nairobi—the capital city—and we had to wait for our materials for a few days, which put us behind on our timeline.

Had you done voluntary work before?

When I was in secondary school, I used to go to Tijuana, Mexico and
40 build houses in the **slums**. That's when I first fell in love with volunteering and helping others, and that's when I realized how little it actually takes to make a difference in other people's lives.

If young people want to get involved in helping people abroad, what advice would you give them?

45 The advice I would give someone who's interested in getting involved with an organization is to choose an organization that fits closely with their own personal beliefs.

What are your plans for the future?

I hope to carry on with ROTH as long as I can. I'd love to keep travelling
50 and building more projects. However, I know that I'll have to go back to school eventually. I'd like to gain more expertise in international development so that I can take ROTH even further.

What impact is ROTH having here in Québec?

ROTH is having a positive impact here in Québec. Most
55 of our volunteers still come from Québec, and over twenty-five Québécois were present for the construction of the Piave Maternity Ward and Counselling Centre in Kenya during the summer of 2007. We have since partnered with secondary schools in the Montréal area
60 and hope to start an exchange program with the girls from the school we built in Tanzania.

Smart Words

afford: be able to pay
aware: knowing about a situation
surroundings: environment
foreigner: a person from another country
slum: district inhabited by very poor people

● Underline the word or expression that does not belong in each group of words.

1. <u>Italy</u>   Tanzania   Kenya   Uganda   South Africa

2. help   volunteer   scream   improve   make a difference

3. wonderful   animals   great sites   Kenya   dangerous

4. candies   shelter   education   nutrition   health care

5. founder   twenty-six   Québec   sick   young woman

● Answer these comprehension questions without looking at the text again. They are not in order.

1. How many volunteers work for Roth?

_____

2. When did Frédérique Vallières start volunteering?

_____

3. What were some of the obstacles in Kenya?

_____

4. Where do most of the volunteers come from?

_____

5. What will you be doing when you are twenty-six?

_____

- Compare what you know about Québec with what Frédérique says about Kenya.

- Complete the chart.

What Frédérique says about Kenya	What I know about Québec
– *People are wonderful.*	– *People are wonderful.*

Work with Grammar

MODALS

Modals are auxiliary verbs used with a main verb. Modals give extra meaning to the verb.

- Underline these modals in the text: *can, could, have to, had to, would.*
  (Look for the contraction.)

- Read the rules and fill in the examples.
  Use *can* or *could* for capability. People _____ make a change.
  Use *should* for advice. Companies _____ waste less.
  Use *may* or *might* for possibility. You _____ see a big difference.
  Use *must* or *have to* for obligation. Teenagers _____ be informed.

- Imagine that you are in Kenya volunteering. Write three things you can or could do to help others. *I could teach children English.*

  1. _____.

  2. _____.

  3. _____.

See Grammar Workshop 5.1 on page 141 for more practice.

6 Write your own interview with someone who is making an impact.

Think about a person you know or someone you heard about who is doing something to change people's lives. It could be something small that is making people happy locally or something that you saw on the news.

- Look at the interview on page 130 for a model and ideas.

STEP 1 Prepare

- Write four questions you want to ask this person.

1. _____

2. _____

3. _____

4. _____

STEP 2 Write

- Write the answers to your questions. Make sure your answers are complete and informative.

1. _____
   _____
   _____

2. _____
   _____
   _____

3. _____
   _____
   _____

4. _____
   _____
   _____

STEP 3 Revise and Edit

- Reread your interview. Are your questions and answers clear?
- Check spelling and grammar. Did you use modals correctly?
- Ask a classmate to look at your work and comment.

STEP 4 Publish

- Write the final version of your interview on a separate sheet of paper.

7 Discover a new way of banking.

Even banks are making changes. The text you will read is a feature article about a man who is changing the way we loan money to create changes.

- **Before you read, answer this question: If you were given $1000 to help someone, how would you use the money?**

_____

A feature article is a news article that goes into a topic in depth. Components include:

headline: main title that grabs your attention

subheadline: sentence(s) giving an idea about the topic of the article

subheading: smaller title of a section that tells you the topic

quote: important phrase from the article that is separated from the regular text and in a bigger font

picture: photo or illustration that helps the reader "see" the situation more clearly

caption: sentence under a photo explaining the picture

- **Look at this feature article and identify the components.**
- **Write the name of each component in the margin next to the article.**
- **While you read, take notes on the differences between a regular bank and Dr. Yunus's bank.**

Headline ●⟶ # An Exceptional Banker

Do you need money?
Yunus will not give YOU any!

1 Muhammad Yunus, a Bangladeshi banker and economist, found a way to help more than 100 million people around the globe step out of
5 poverty. He is famous for providing micro-credit—small loans—to the poor, especially women.

> "Your money will be recycled again and again. Much greater
10 impact can be derived from it than from charity."

How it started

Dr. Yunus, the third of nine children, was born in Bangladesh,
15 one of the poorest countries in the world. His mother, who

Muhammad Yunus of Bangladesh, the 2006 Nobel Peace Prize winner, speaks in Stockholm, Sweden

▶ always helped the poor, first inspired him to dedicate his life to the **eradication** of poverty. When he started teaching, his country was experiencing a famine. He saw so much suffering that he felt he had
20 to do something to change people's lives.

He found that if you **loan** the poor the small amounts of money they need, they can often help themselves out of poverty. One day, he lent $27 to a group of bamboo weavers in a local village. (It was simply the money he had in his pocket.) He remembers how excited the people
25 were. The **borrowers** were really grateful for the money, and they paid back the loan shortly after. Dr. Yunus decided to continue lending money with no interest. This was how he founded Grameen Bank (which means "village bank").

What is the bank doing now?

30 Grameen Bank has now lent over $11 billion to people all over Bangladesh. Because Dr. Yunus decided to take action, the lives of families and small entrepreneurs are changing one by one. Loans are given only to the very poorest. Borrowers in Bangladesh must demonstrate that their families own less than half an acre of land.

35 **Why it works**

You might think that people borrow large amounts of money, but the average loan is only $130. Dr. Yunus calls it *micro-credit*. Because the money is loaned and not given, people know that they will have to pay it back. Therefore, they borrow only what they really need. As a
40 result, 99 percent of the borrowers pay back their loans, and 58 percent of them can finally get out of poverty. Surprisingly, 96 percent of the borrowers are women. They use the money to launch businesses. If women have money, then their children will eat better, have better clothes and go to school. Dr. Yunus believes that the right to credit
45 should be recognized as a fundamental human right.

Dr. Yunus is convinced that what he is doing is better than charity. "Your money will be recycled again and again. Much greater impact can be derived from it than from charity. The charity dollar has only one life; you give and it never comes back."[1]

50 **How he is influencing others**

According to a government expert, the micro-credit program established by Dr. Yunus is the single most important development in the Third World in the last 100 years. His methods are now applied in projects in fifty-eight countries, including the United States, Canada,
55 France, the Netherlands and Norway.

Dr. Yunus and Grameen Bank have received several national and international honours, including the Nobel Peace Prize. He is also the author of *Banker to the Poor* and *Creating a World Without Poverty*. He hopes that we can one day have a poverty museum.

---

1. Dr. Muhammad Yunus, quoted by Alison Benjamin, "Money Well Lent," *The Guardian, Global development*, June 2, 2009. Web. Feb. 6, 2012.

Smart **Words**

eradication: elimination

verb: _____

loan: lend

noun: _____

borrower: person who takes money from a bank under an agreement to pay it back later

verb: _____

Notes

_____
_____
_____
_____
_____
_____
_____
_____
_____
_____

Name: _____ Group: _____ Date: _____

- After you read, write the noun or verb for each of the Smart Words. You may need to use a dictionary.
- Complete this chart comparing a regular bank and Dr. Yunus's bank.
- Use your notes to help you.

A regular bank	Dr. Yunus's bank
– Lends money to everyone. – Makes a lot of profit.	

- Answer these questions.

1. How do women use the money they borrow?

_____

2. What is "micro-credit"?

_____

3. How does the text describe Bangladesh?

_____

4. Who inspired Dr. Yunus to help the poor?

_____

5. What percentage of people get out of poverty?

_____

Work with Grammar

CONNECTIVES

- Circle these connectives in the text: *so … that, because* and *therefore*.

People are connected by actions: what one person does can have an effect on others. Connectives help you to express cause and effect, contrast and conditions for such actions.

Look at these examples.
Because *the speech was powerful, people decided to help.*
The humanitarian help didn't arrive on time. **Therefore**, *people died.*
The organization is **so** *popular* **that** *it needs new volunteers all the time.*

- Complete these sentences.

Grameen Bank is great because _____

Mr. Yunus helps women. Therefore, _____

Mr. Yunus's idea was so good that _____

See Grammar Workshop 5.2 on page 143 for more practice.

8 Find out how we are all connected.

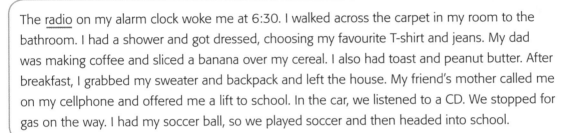

Many of us feel that we can't help people in other countries because they are so far away from us. In this activity, you will learn how our lives and actions are closely connected with those of other people around the globe.

- Read the following paragraph about a typical Canadian student's morning.

- Underline the products that you have at home and that you think are made in or come from another country.

> The radio on my alarm clock woke me at 6:30. I walked across the carpet in my room to the bathroom. I had a shower and got dressed, choosing my favourite T-shirt and jeans. My dad was making coffee and sliced a banana over my cereal. I also had toast and peanut butter. After breakfast, I grabbed my sweater and backpack and left the house. My friend's mother called me on my cellphone and offered me a lift to school. In the car, we listened to a CD. We stopped for gas on the way. I had my soccer ball, so we played soccer and then headed into school.

- Listen to the audio segment and identify the countries mentioned and the impact the products have on the world.

 You can try an extra listening activity using this text on the Companion Website.

- Complete the chart below.

Product	Countries Involved in Bringing the Product to Canada	Impact on the World
Alarm clock	*China*, *Brazil*, Greece, Sweden, Liberia, Portugal	– Not mentioned
Carpet	India	–
Shower products	United Kingdom	– _____ – tries to reduce wasteful packaging
Shirt	_____, Haiti	– Workers work for one or _____. – They are exposed to _____. – They have no access to _____. – Women earn _____.
Peanuts		– Workers receive _____ of what we pay in the grocery store.
Coffee		
Sugar		
Bananas		
Sweater	Not mentioned	– The company _____.

FINAL TASK

C3 9 Write a feature article.

You have read about different projects that are changing the world and thought about how you, too, could change your community. Write a feature article about a great project you heard about or choose one of these three topics.

1. A student in your school is raising awareness of the lack of handicapped access in your school: ten students will go around your school for one day in wheelchairs.

2. A group of students at your school has decided to raise funds to help the victims of a natural disaster.

3. A student in your school is raising money and food donations for the local food bank after seeing a homeless man begging for food on the street.

● **Read the model feature article on page 134 to help you.**

STEP 1 Prepare

● **Choose the topic of your feature article or do some research to find an idea.**

● **Search the Internet, read magazines and talk to people you know to help you.**

● **Answer these questions.**

Who is the hero of this article? _____

What is the project? _____

Who is the person helping and how? _____

_____

What are the strong points of the project? _____

_____

Does the project face any obstacles? _____

_____

How can more people participate? _____

_____

STEP 2 Write

● **Write the text. Give details.**

Headline: _____

Subheadline: _____

Introduction: (Write a summary of the person and the project.) _____

_____

_____

_____

Picture: (Describe it.) _____

Caption: _____

Subheading 1: *How it started* _____

_____

_____

_____

Subheading 2: *What she/he is doing now* _____

_____

_____

Subheading 3: *Why it works* _____

_____

_____

_____

Subheading 4: *Obstacles to overcome* _____

_____

_____

Subheading 5: *How people can participate* _____

_____

_____

_____

STEP 3 Revise and Edit

- Is your message clear? Does it include the characteristics of a feature article?
- Did you use modal auxiliaries? Did you use connectives correctly?
- Ask a classmate to look at your text and comment.

Name of the person who reviewed my text: _____

Comments and suggestions: _____

STEP 4 Publish

- Write the final version of your feature article on a separate sheet of paper.

⁙WRAP-UP

Try an extra activity using vocabulary from this unit on the Companion Website.

Test Your **S**marts

- Look at these words and make connections.
- Share them with a partner. Make sure you can justify your connections.

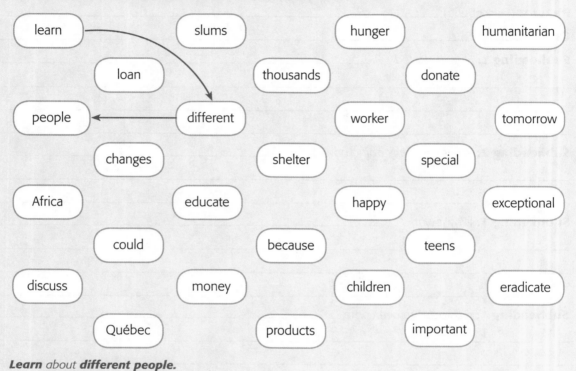

learn	slums		hunger		humanitarian
loan		thousands		donate	
people	different		worker		tomorrow
changes		shelter		special	
Africa	educate		happy		exceptional
could		because		teens	
discuss	money		children		eradicate
Québec		products		important	

*Learn about **different people.***

Smart **Expressions**

- Look at the following expressions about world action.
- Choose the best definition for each one.

Mateo ***put his heart and soul into*** this project. He really believes in it.

They worked ***hand in hand*** with the local population.

1. When you put your heart and soul into something, you

  a) are very enthusiastic about it.   b) give all your money to it.   c) cry all the time.

2. When people work hand in hand, they

  a) hold hands.   b) work together closely.   c) lack cooperation.

- Think of your own life and write a sentence using one of these expressions.

_____

_____

GRAMMAR WORKSHOP 5.1

Modals

What do you know?

Do you know how to use modals?

Example: In my summer job, I **could** do everything my boss asked me to do.

- Match each sentence with the correct function of the modal being used.
- Check your answers at the bottom of the page.

   Example: After years of study, he could now work in the developing world. _(d)_

1. I could offer you a job if you need to make money. ◯

2. May I ask you if you are interested in making a donation? ◯

3. We might go to Peru to work in an orphanage. ◯

4. Sally has to finish high school before she can go to Nepal. ◯

5. Tim will work for a year as a doctor in a remote community. ◯

Function

a) permission

b) obligation

c) promise

d) capability

e) possibility

Score: _____/5

Rules

- Review the rules for using modals in the chart below.

Modals		
Function	Modals	Example
Possibility	may, might	I **might** take your advice.
Capability	can, could	I **could** lower my tone of voice.
Permission	may, can	**Can** I forward this e-mail?
Suggestion/Advice	should	You **shouldn't** talk with your mouth full.
Obligation	must, have to	You **have to** follow these rules.
Intention/Promise	will	I **will** try to change my behaviour.
Politeness	would, could	**Would** you help me, please?

Answers: 1-d, capability; 2-a, permission; 3-e, possibility; 4-b, obligation; 5-c, promise

Practice

Exercise 1

- Underline the correct modal for each sentence.

Example: (<u>May</u> / Would) I help you with the fundraiser planning?

1. Volunteering in Mexico is exciting! You (would / should) come along!

2. You (may / could) spend your summer at home, but you (could / may) never have this opportunity again.

3. I (would / could) talk to Steve if I were you.

4. He (might / can) have some information from his trip last summer that (could / must) help you make up your mind.

5. There is a slight chance that I (may / can) convince my parents to let me go as well!

6. It (would / should) be awesome if we went together.

Exercise 2

- Rewrite each sentence using the correct modal to express possibility, obligation or advice.

Example: Julie is organizing a fundraiser for the local shelter.

Possibility: *Julie may/might organize a fundraiser.*
Obligation: *Julie must / has to organize a fundraiser.*
Advice: *Julie should organize a fundraiser.*

1. Steve and I are researching aid agencies that need volunteers.

Possibility: _____
Obligation: _____
Advice: _____

2. Mary is campaigning to beautify the campus.

Possibility: _____
Advice: _____
Obligation: _____

3. Alfred is going to Chile to build houses.

Obligation: _____
Possibility: _____
Advice: _____

Name: _____ Group: _____ Date: _____

Exercise 3

- Using the modals in parentheses, write four tips for getting involved and making changes in your school or community.

   Example: (could) *You could start a new club at your school to address an important issue.*

(should) _____
_____

(must) _____
_____

(could) _____
_____

(can) _____
_____

GRAMMAR WORKSHOP 5.2

Connectives

What do you know?

Do you know how to use connectives?

Example: The donations poured in after the earthquake **because** people understood there was lot of damage.

- Complete each sentence with the correct connective.
- Check your answers at the bottom of the page.

> despite   therefore   otherwise   however   so that   ~~because~~

Example: Roxanne helps out in the soup kitchen ___*because*___ she thinks it's the right thing to do.

1. The road to the village was dangerous. _____, it was difficult to deliver the food supplies on time.
2. Jim has to be on the next plane to Tibet. _____, he will miss the chance to volunteer for this project.
3. We held many fundraisers _____ we could spend the summer in Zimbabwe building a school.
4. The villagers survived the cold winter _____ having very little food to eat.
5. The aid workers delivered the seeds and water pumps to the village; _____, the villagers still missed the planting season.

Score: _____/5

Answers: 1-therefore; 2-otherwise; 3-so that; 4-despite; 5-however

Rules

● Review the rules for using connectives in the chart below.

Connectives		
When	Connectives	Examples
Cause and effect	because because of therefore consequently such…that so…that so that since due to so	People decided to get involved **because** the director's speech was so persuasive. **Because of** the delay, we cannot start the project. Humanitarian aid didn't arrive. **Therefore / Consequently**, people died. The weather is **so** bad **that** the roads are closed. The food bank is open seven days a week **so that** people in need can come any time. The delay in supplies is **due to** the bad weather.
Contrast of ideas	even though despite nevertheless although but however anyway	**Even though** it was a great initiative, it didn't work out. They raised a lot of money **despite** all the organizational problems. Thousands of people participated in the rally. **Nevertheless**, they didn't raise enough money. The fundraisers are disappointed, **but** they won't give up. **However**, they will try something different next time.
Conditions	otherwise or else	Fortunately, the community gives to our local food bank. **Otherwise**, some people would go hungry. The children need school uniforms, **or else** they can't go to school.

COMPANION
web+
Try extra grammar exercises for connectives on the Companion Website.

Practice

Exercise 1

● Match the first part of the sentence with the correct connective.

Example: My parents were nervous	*f*	**a.**	**because** she won the prize for raising the most money at the fundraiser.
❶ She was happy		**b.**	**so** he was late arriving at the planning meeting.
❷ He missed the bus,		**c.**	**because of** the disturbing images used in the presentation.
❸ The fundraising picnic was cancelled		**d.**	**due to** the different position of the steering wheel.
❹ I couldn't concentrate during the information session for the trip to Africa		**e.**	**since** it was raining.
❺ She didn't hear her alarm clock;		**f.**	**because** it was the first time I had ever travelled without them.
❻ The store manager sponsored the event		**g.**	**consequently**, she missed her flight to Mexico.
❼ Driving in India was difficult		**h.**	**so that** the students could visit the school in Kenya.

Exercise 2

- Underline the connectives.

Sebastian had a great year <u>because of</u> his memorable experiences as a volunteer worker. Due to his useful skills, he had the opportunity to go to Bolivia. Even though it was difficult at the beginning, he was able to reach out to local children. Despite the many challenges he faced, he decided to stay abroad. Otherwise, he knew he would regret it. Because he did such a great job, Sebastian has been invited to go to Kenya next year. He is so excited about his work that he has asked his brother to come along, too.

Exercise 3

- Complete each sentence by underlining the correct connective.

Example: (<u>Even though</u> / But) I was nervous, I spoke about my volunteer experience in front of a hundred teens and their parents.

1. Skip had to sign up for the humanitarian trip, (or else / otherwise) he would have regretted not going.

2. After our flight home, we slept for twelve hours. (Although / Nevertheless), we still felt jet-lagged.

3. I was chosen to go on the humanitarian trip (even though / nevertheless) I hadn't raised much money to cover the costs.

4. Terry went to the protest rally (despite / even though) being sick.

5. This country receives a lot of aid, (but / despite) it is still very poor.

6. Christophe knew that they had to raise $70 000, (or else / even though) they would be forced to close the community centre.

7. My parents want me to go to college in the fall. (However / Although), I want to do a year of humanitarian work abroad instead.

8. I want to find a cure for AIDS. (Therefore / Even so), I have decided to study science at university.

Exercise 4

- Write a short paragraph explaining why you want to travel.

- Include two connectives.

_____

_____

_____

_____

_____

_____

READING WORKSHOP 5

Compare and Contrast

When you compare, you consider two things and find similarities and differences.

When you contrast, you consider two things and highlight differences.

Let's look at two texts about peacemakers.

Before You Read

- **Look at the internal and external features (titles, subtitles, pictures, audience, topics) of each text.**

- **What similarities and differences do you notice between the two texts?**

   1. What are the topics of the texts?

   Text 1: _____ Text 2: _____

   2. Are these topics similar or different? Explain why.

   _____

   _____

   _____

   3. What do the subtitles tell you?

   _____

   _____

   _____

   4. How are these subtitles similar and different?

   _____

   _____

   _____

While You Read

- **Fill in the Venn diagram on page 147 to explore the similarities and differences between the two texts.**

- **Note elements the two men have in common in the middle of the diagram and their differences in the circles.**

Nelson Mandela

- *was not part of (white) ruling class*

Similarities

- *changed the political system of their countries*

Mahatma Gandhi

- *was part of ruling class (father was a prime minister)*

Nelson Mandela

Peacemaker and Nobel Prize winner

Rolihlahla ("Troublemaker") Mandela, later named Nelson Mandela, was born in Transkei, South Africa, on July 18, 1918. He is a member of the Tembu tribe, a Xhosa tribe that is part of the Nguni people.
5 His father was Chief Henry Mandela of the Tembu.

For most of Mandela's life, the South African government supported a political system known as *apartheid*. Apartheid **dictated** the lives of non-whites down to the last detail—where they worked, where they lived, even where they died. This oppressive racist regime was condemned around the world.

10 Influenced by Mahatma Gandhi, Mandela was initially committed to non-violent resistance against apartheid. However, he grew **disillusioned** by the lack of progress toward equality for non-whites.

In 1942, Mandela joined the armed wing of the African National Congress (ANC) to fight against apartheid. He had decided that armed **struggle** was the only way to create
15 a mutiracial democracy.

Twenty years later, Mandela was arrested for his connection to ANC violence against apartheid. On June 12, 1964, he was sentenced to life imprisonment.

At the age of seventy-two, Mandela was set free, after serving twenty-eight years. It was February 11, 1990. The following year, he was elected president of the ANC, and three years
20 later, he became the country's first non-white democratically elected president.

Smart Words

dictate: insist forcefully

disillusioned: disappointed because of lost beliefs

struggle: fight

Following his release from prison, Mandela worked toward a peaceful reconciliation between whites and non-whites. In 1993, Mandela was awarded the Nobel Peace Prize along with then-South African President Frederik Willem de Klerk. The two men—one black, one white—were jointly accorded the
25 honour "for their work for the peaceful termination of the apartheid regime, and for laying the foundations for a new democratic South Africa."

Mahatma Gandhi

1 **Peacemaker but not a Nobel Prize winner**

Mahatma ("Great Soul") Gandhi, born Mohandas Gandhi, became the strongest symbol of non-violence in the twentieth century. Many people believe that the Indian national leader should
5 have been selected for the Nobel Peace Prize. He was nominated a number of times: 1937, 1938, 1939, 1947 and again just days before his murder in 1948. He was never awarded the prize.

Born in 1869 in Porbandar in the west of India, Gandhi was named Mohandas Karamchand by his father, who served as diwan (prime minister) to the King of Rajkot. The rich Gandhi
10 family belonged to a **devout** branch of Hinduism that advocated non-violence and tolerance among religious groups.

Gandhi moved to South Africa at the age of twenty-four. While he was there, he tried to improve living conditions for the Indian minority. He successfully introduced a strategy of non-violence and peaceful protest into the South African Indians' struggle for basic human
15 rights.

Smart Words

devout: very religious

partitioning: dividing

When he returned to India in 1915, Gandhi began a series of non-violent campaigns of civil disobedience against the British colonial authorities. At the same time, he championed efforts to unite Indian Hindus, Muslims and Christians.

20 During the last months of his life, Gandhi worked tirelessly for an end to the violence between Hindus and Muslims that had followed the **partitioning** of India into India and Pakistan. In 1948, he was assassinated during his nightly walk by a Hindu radical.

After You Read

- Use a T-chart to contrast the texts and select two of the main differences between them.

Text about Mandela	Text about Gandhi
Mandela	Gandhi
• *was a black South African*	• *was an Indian*
• *was poor*	• *was rich*
_____	_____
_____	_____
_____	_____

- Answer the questions about both texts.

1. What was apartheid?

_____

_____

_____

2. Why was Mandela arrested?

_____

_____

3. How many years was Mandela in prison?

_____

4. What did Mandela do when he came out of prison?

_____

_____

_____

5. What does the name "Mahatma" mean?

_____

6. How many times was Gandhi nominated for the Nobel Peace Prize?

_____

7. Where did Gandhi first work to improve the living conditions of Indians?

_____

8. What method did Gandhi introduce in the struggle for human rights?

_____

WRITING WORKSHOP 5

Feature Article

Feature articles are detailed pieces of writing written from the point of view of the writer in order to inform or entertain the reader. This means they often take an interesting angle on a topic, causing you to react.

Unlike news articles or reports, which can quickly go out of date, feature articles do not. Instead they focus on popular issues and topics of general interest.

A feature article includes a headline, sometimes a subheadline, an introduction, a main body and a conclusion.

Let's look at these components one at a time.

Headline

Many feature articles have both a headline and a subheadline.

– Headline: This can be made up of a word, a phrase, even a sentence, as long as it is intriguing and grabs the reader's attention.

– Subheadline: This is typically written in smaller letters than the headline and bigger letters than the text. Often it has a different font from the text. It should give the reader an idea about the topic of the article.

Community Work Fits "Mr. Optimism"
Elias Moukannas serves numerous organizations—with a smile.

- Write a catchy headline and a subheadline for a feature article you will write later on volunteer work.

  Headline: _____

  Subheadline: _____

  _____

- Underline the best headline below. Explain why you chose it.

  1. Volunteer Work and Its Advantages

  2. A Job That Will Not Feel Like a Job!

  3. Helping Others Is Good

  _____

  _____

- Look at the headline you wrote. Is it catchy? Will a reader want to know more about volunteer work? If not, try again.

_____

_____

- Underline the best subheadline. Explain why you chose it.

  1. Volunteer workers are so happy that they don't feel they're working.

  2. Volunteer workers do not get paid and are disappointed.

  3. There are millions of volunteer workers around the world.

_____

_____

- Look at the subheadline you wrote. Does it give the reader an idea about the topic of volunteer work? If not, try again.

_____

Introduction

An introduction makes up the first paragraph. It outlines the topic or theme of the article.

- **Read the introduction below.**

It's a good thing Elias Moukannas was given a big, bright smile, because the man people call "Mr. Optimism" is seldom without one. Elias spreads sunshine wherever he goes. He is involved with no less than six different organizations.

- **Write a check mark beside the characteristics that are included in this introduction.**

  an unusual statement ◯

  background information ◯

  an opinion ◯

Main Body

The main body of a feature article addresses the how and why of the topic. Divided into subtopics, it consists of detailed paragraphs that may contain the following:

– **Facts and statistics:** These give your readers confidence and support your point of view. Double-check their accuracy.

– **Images:** Photographs and images make a text more interesting. Keep track of where you found them.

– **Captions:** These short bits of text explain an image and are placed close to it. If people are present in the image, the caption includes their full names.

– Quotes: Quotations are the accurate recordings of a person's words. By using quotation marks (" ") , you are telling the reader that the words are not yours.

– Sidebars: These are usually framed separately from the main body. Typically made up of a paragraph with a heading, they include information that is related but not essential to the article. They may also include images.

- Read the opening section of the feature article below.

- Locate each of the following components in the article and write their names in the correct place in the margin next to the article.

> caption   fact   opinion   photograph   quote   statistic

The Long Road Home

In Haiti, families struggle to return to normal even years after the earthquake.

Pierre Henri, 53, thinks about what he has lost. The office where he once worked is closed. His block is full of wrecked homes, many abandoned. A pile of debris sits in front of what used to be Pierre's house.

"I cried when I saw my house destroyed," he says, remembering the first time he returned home after the earthquake.

Pierre and his wife Joanne, 45, have lived in a tent since then. But he still feels lucky when he thinks about the 316 000 people who died.

The tent where Pierre and Joanne Henri have been living since the earthquake

Conclusion

The last paragraph of a feature article reminds the reader of the main topic. It may suggest a solution or encourage readers to change their minds. It may also include a final quote, a summary statement, a warning or an indirect reference to the headline of the article.

- Read the conclusion on the next page.

The country has begun to recover. More houses are finished every day. However, this does not help Pierre Henri or the other half million people who are still homeless and living in tents. They hope that the world has not forgotten them now that Haiti is no longer in the news. If not, their long road home will become even longer.

- Write a check mark beside the characteristics that are included in this conclusion.

  ◯ a summary statement

  ◯ a reminder of the main topic

  ◯ a warning or an indirect reference to the headline of the article

It's Your Turn

- Write a feature article about volunteer work, using your headline and subheadline.
- Use as many connectives and modals as possible.
- Brainstorm the content of your article.
- Write a rough copy of the introduction.

_____
_____
_____
_____
_____

Checklist

◯ Have you outlined the topic or theme of the article?

◯ Have you provided any necessary background information?

◯ Have you included an unusual statement?

◯ Have you included an opinion?

- Write a rough copy of the main body of your feature article. Write two paragraphs.

Paragraph 1

Subheading: _____

Text: _____
_____
_____
_____
_____
_____

▶

Paragraph 2

Subheading: _____

Text: _____

_____

_____

_____

_____

_____

Checklist

◯ Have you included a subheading for each paragraph?

◯ Have you included at least one quote?

◯ Have you included at least one statistic?

◯ Have you included at least two facts?

◯ Have you included at least one opinion?

● Decide on an image for your story. Who and/or what would be in the picture? Describe it.

_____

_____

_____

● Reread your article and underline the most pertinent sentence. When you write your final copy, make it stand out by changing it to a subheadline.

● Write a rough copy of the conclusion to your feature article.

_____

_____

_____

_____

_____

Checklist

◯ Did you remind the reader of the main topic?

◯ Did you suggest a solution?

◯ Did you encourage the reader to agree with you?

● Write a final copy of your feature article on a separate piece of paper.

How true are urban legends?

Urban legends are a special kind of story because they are almost believable, are entertaining and usually try to scare us.

● **Complete the word banks by grouping these words into synonyms.**

alarm	fabrication	fiction	joke	trick	upset
bluff	fib	frighten	scam	untruth	worry

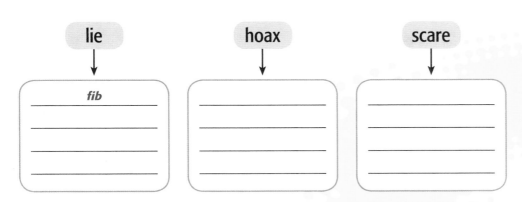

lie

fib

hoax

scare

SMART START

1 Is it fact or fiction?

Some stories sound either too good to be true or too ridiculous to believe. Can you tell the difference? Take this quiz to see if you can spot the truth.

- Work with a partner to decide if the statements are fact or fiction.
- Calculate your score. Your teacher will provide the explanations.

Statements	Fact	Fiction
❶ You can fry an egg on the sidewalk in extremely warm weather.		
❷ When you bite a Wint-O-Green Lifesaver in the dark, it makes a spark.		
❸ If you leave a nail in a glass of cola for four days, it will dissolve.		
❹ You can stop a can of soda from bubbling if you tap the side of the can before you open it.		
❺ If you swallow gum, it will stay in your stomach for seven years.		
❻ If you tie enough helium-filled balloons to your body, you will fly.		
❼ The average person eats six spiders a year in their sleep.		
❽ Jell-O gelatin contains animal bones and skin.		

Add up the points: _____

Smart Talk

I don't believe it, because …

I think the story sounds too good to be true.

What makes you think …?

Can you explain what you mean by …?

Interpret the score

8 correct answers:

Sally the Sleuth!
You can spot a fib from a mile away. You never waste time thinking about whether a story is true or false, you just know the difference. Either that or you're just a lucky guesser.

5 to 7 correct answers:

Reasonable Ryan!
You can't always tell fact from fiction, but you know better than to believe everything you read, see or hear. You are most likely to research a story that you aren't sure about.

0 to 4 correct answers:

Gullible Gary!
Unfortunately, you believe just about any tale you are told. You need to research your facts a bit more and get to the bottom of a story before you believe it. You're probably the one spreading these crazy stories around.

2 How can you spot an urban legend?

There are a few tricks you can use to help spot an urban legend when you hear or read one. We wish we could tell you they are foolproof, but, as you will read, sometimes crazy stories turn out to be true.

A ● Find each Smart Word in the text.

● Read the complete sentence to better understand the context.

● Write a new sentence with each Smart Word.

believable: _____

reliable: _____

word of mouth: _____

validity: _____

dead giveaway: _____

● Read the tricks in the text below.

How to Spot an Urban Legend

1 Urban legends are just **believable** enough that you may not always be able to spot the ones that aren't true. They usually come from a source that we feel is **reliable**, either via e-mail or by **word of mouth**. These two factors make us not think twice about the **validity** of a story.

5 Here are a few questions that can usually help you to spot an urban legend:

❶ Did the story happen to a friend of a friend (FOAF)? If the answer is YES, then this could be an urban legend. This is a key urban legend technique. The story didn't happen to the person telling it to you, but you really trust them. They definitely trust the person who told them
10 the story too, because they are now telling it to you, right?

❷ Are the details of the story specific and easily verifiable? If not, then this is a clue that the story might be an urban legend. For example, the fact that a city or an institution is never named should be a **dead giveaway**. Names make a story seem authentic, but check them out.
15 Sometimes you just need to look carefully or say them aloud to realize that they are fake.

❸ Does the story have an important message or teach a valuable lesson? If the answer is yes, it may be an urban legend. Urban legends are used to try to scare people into being good or acting in a certain way.

20 ❹ Does the story sound too good or too silly to be true? If so, then this could be an urban legend.

Smart Words

believable: seems possible

reliable: can be trusted

word of mouth: one person telling another

validity: level of truth

dead giveaway: obvious

B ● Read the two stories.

● Use the tricks to determine if the stories are true.

Story 1

> Our church has just banned people from throwing rice at weddings. Apparently it kills birds. Here is the flyer they handed out.

Attention Parishioners!

Because of a <u>very</u> disturbing event that happened a few weeks ago during a wedding at St. Bruno's church on 45th Street,[2] we ask that you no longer throw rice as the bride and groom leave the church.

We know that this has been a tradition at our church for a fairly long time, but it seems it is extremely unsafe for birds. According to Reid Enright, a bird researcher at the local university, birds eat the rice and then drink a little water. The really scary part is that the rice expands, and if the birds eat a lot of rice, they could definitely explode. Sadly, this is fairly common and is what happened at the St. Bruno church wedding.

The church staff are extremely concerned for the well-being of the local wildlife, and so we ask you to use bubbles to shower the bride and groom as they leave the church. This will also reduce the workload for our janitor, who is left to clean up any leftover rice.

Story 2

From: Ryan
To: Sally
Subject: Wire BBQ cleaning brush alert

Hi Sally,

This is really awful—it happened to a friend of my cousin at a BBQ recently.

The owner of the BBQ used an old metal brush to clean the grill, and one of the wire **bristles** came off. Somehow, the wire bristle got stuck in my cousin's friend's hamburger, and when he ate it, it got stuck in his throat. The friend was very lucky he didn't choke and die, but he did have to go to the emergency room and have the wire surgically removed. Isn't that gross? I'm definitely going to check my hamburgers in future.

The doctor said it is extremely important that you change your cleaning brush regularly and always wipe the grill with a cloth before putting food on it.

Forward this e-mail to all your BBQing friends.

Smart **Words**

bristle: short hair, usually made of plastic or metal, on a brush

● Read the stories again and identify sections of the text that match the tricks for spotting an urban legend on page 157.

● Write the number of the corresponding trick beside each section.

● Decide if these statements are true or false. If the statement is false, write the correct statement.

	True	False
❶ Birds died because people attending a wedding threw rice at them. **Correction: Birds ate the rice and it expanded in their stomachs, making them explode.**		✓
❷ The story of the exploding birds is an urban legend.		
❸ If a story starts with "A friend of a friend …" it is always an urban legend.		
❹ A good way to spot an urban legend is to look for specific details that you can verify.		
❺ The cleaning brush got stuck in the hamburger that the cousin's friend ate.		
❻ The BBQ story really happened.		

Work with Grammar

INTENSIFIERS

Intensifiers are adverbs that enhance adjectives, verbs and other adverbs. In urban legends, they exaggerate details and make them seem more important, scary or true. Here are some examples:

a little	extremely	rather	relatively	totally
definitely	fairly	really	too	very

● **Scan the two stories and underline the intensifiers.**

● **Complete the following rule.**

In English, intensifiers come _____ the words they modify.

Incorrect: *Sharron checks definitely all the e-mail stories she receives.*

Correct: *Sharron definitely checks all the e-mail stories she receives.*

● **Fill in the blanks with different intensifiers. See the list above.**

Ms. Fordparker, our English teacher, tells _____ great urban legends. Her stories are _____ believable, so it is _____ hard to tell if they are true or false. She tells the stories _____ well and we enjoy hearing them.

See Grammar Workshop 6.1 on page 173 for more practice.

 3 Have you heard the one about …?

Urban legends tend to sound a bit crazy and confusing. One way to keep track of what is happening in the story is to note the main story elements, such as setting, characters and action. Also keep in mind that many urban legends end at the most exciting point in the story.

- **Before you listen, read the Smart Words and their definitions.**

- **While you listen, use the story chart to note the important elements of each story.**

Try an extra listening activity using this text on the Companion Website.

Smart Words

Klingon: language developed through the television show *Star Trek*

persist: continue to spread

overbake: cook too much

tan: stay in the sun until your skin darkens in colour

crispy: pleasantly hard on the outside

Story 1: Overbaked

Introduction:
Characters: Young girl, _____
_____

Setting: _____

Story Events:
Girl goes to a tanning salon. _____
_____
_____
_____
_____
_____
_____
_____

Climax:
_____
_____
_____
_____
_____
_____

Story 2: The Hook

Story Events:
– *Two teenagers go to a hill above town in a car to kiss.*
_____
_____
_____
_____

Introduction:
Characters: _____
_____
_____
Setting: _____
_____
_____

Climax:
They get out of the car and find a bloody
hook in the door of the car.
_____
_____
_____

Smart Words

gory: disturbing and unpleasant
hook: curved piece of metal

Work with Grammar

PAST PROGRESSIVE TENSE

The past progressive tense is used to describe actions in the past that happened over a period of time or that were taking place when another action happened.

- **Listen to the interview again and identify these examples.**

   1. *But this poor girl **wasn't getting** tanned fast enough …*

   2. *While they **were kissing** with the radio on, the music was suddenly interrupted.*

   3. *… but she **was feeling** uneasy and finally demanded that he take her home.*

- **Fill in the blanks to complete the rule.**

   To form the past progressive tense we use *was / were* + _____ + _____.

- **Read the complete chart and complete the examples of the past progressive tense.**

Affirmative	Negative	Question
❶ She _____ to get a tan.	❶ She _____ trying to get a tan.	❶ _____ to get a tan?
❷ You were e-mailing scary stories.	❷ You _____ e-mailing scary stories.	❷ _____ scary stories?
❸ We _____ an urban legend.	❸ We _____ reading an urban legend.	❸ Were we reading an urban legend?

See Grammar Workshop 6.2 on page 175 for more practice.

4 Write a plan for an urban legend.

Using tools like a plot map and note chart can really help when you are writing short stories, including urban legends.

STEP 1 Prepare

- Complete the story organizer with as many details as you can. You don't have to use all the details you include in your chart, but it will help when you begin to write.

Urban Legend Story Organizer	
Working Title:	

	Key Words and Vocabulary:
❶ Introduction	Research synonyms for words that you may use in the story to create a feeling (really scary, extremely funny, very creepy, rather paranoid …)
a) Setting:	
Where does the story take place? _____ _____	
What time of day is it? _____ _____	
b) Characters:	
Who is in the story? _____ _____	
What do they look like? _____ _____	
Special details about the characters: _____ _____ _____	
❷ Rising action	Notes:
List the story events in the order that they will happen.	
● _____	
● _____	
● _____	
● _____	
● _____	
❸ Climax	
What is the high point in the story?	
How does the story end? Does it end at the climax?	

STEP 2 Write

- Start by writing an introduction paragraph of three to five sentences.

My neighbour's daughter was driving late one night … She was twenty-three years old and had long blond hair and … It was clouding over, but you could still see the full moon …

_____

_____

_____

_____

_____

- Next, write brief sentences describing the rising action.

She is driving and sees a light ahead. She slows down … She sees a woman crying on the side of the road … She stops to help but can't fix the problem …

_____

_____

_____

_____

- Finish your story plan by writing three to five sentences for the climax.

When the officer hears the story, he grows silent. Then he tells the story of Molly May, a young girl who died in a terrible car accident twenty-five years ago at that exact spot. Each year, someone stops to report her, but there's never anyone there …

_____

_____

_____

_____

STEP 3 Revise and Edit

- Reread your plan. Did you include all the important details to complete your story?
- Check spelling and grammar. Did you use intensifiers to make your story more interesting? Did you use the past progressive tense correctly?
- Ask someone to look at your work and comment.

STEP 4 Publish

- Write the final version of your story plan.

5 A reporter exposes the truth.

Many urban legends are about finding strange ingredients in household products. In this video, one man reveals the truth about Tim Horton's coffee.

- Read the Smart Words and definitions before you watch the video.

- While you watch, listen for the answers to the questions.

    1. What did Tim Horton do before establishing his coffee and doughnut shop?

    _____

    2. Tim Horton's now claims that they are more popular than which sport?

    _____

    3. What are the reporter's two main goals with the tests he is doing on the coffee?

    _____

    _____

    _____

    4. If these urban legends are true, what would motivate a company to create a highly caffeinated coffee with nicotine in it?

    _____

    5. What are the results of the coffee test?

    _____

    _____

- Complete the chart with information from the animation of the typical urban legend about Tim Horton's coffee.

Story Events:
1. *The woman drinks a Tim Horton's coffee.*
2. _____
3. _____
4. _____
5. _____
6. _____

Introduction:
Characters: ***Someone's girlfriend's cousin's husband's mother***
_____

Setting: _____

Climax:
_____
_____
_____
_____

Name: _____ Group: _____ Date: _____

6 Travel the World Wide Web.

The Internet and e-mail are helping urban legends spread like wildfire. Researching the Internet is also the fastest way to find information when you are trying to validate or disprove an urban legend.

- **Circle the best answer to complete the sentence.**

- **If you are unsure, find the Smart Word in bold in the text and guess the meaning from the context.**

  1. If a story **goes viral** on the Internet,

     a) nobody reads it.   b) everybody you know reads it.

  2. If something is **a steal of a deal** when you buy it,

     a) it is almost free.   b) it is very expensive.

  3. If you see lots of **maggots** on something,

     a) you should eat it.   b) it is rotten.

  4. If an animal is covered in **feathers**,

     a) it's a bird.   b) it's a fish.

  5. If I find an e-mail **suspect**,

     a) I'm not sure if it is true.   b) I'm positive it is the truth.

  6. If my clothes are **soaked**,

     a) they are warm and dry.   b) they are full of water.

  7. If a nail is **crooked**,

     a) it will go into the wall   b) it will go into the wall
        at an angle.   very straight.

  8. If the **shelf life** of my cookies is long,

     a) I need to eat them quickly.   b) they can last a very long time.

- **While you read, make notes to help you complete the chart on page 167: write a check mark beside information that you think is believable and write an X beside information that you think is made up.**

Express Yourself Plus • **Unit 6** 165

Urban Legends Go Viral on the Net
by Brighton Early

1 Have you ever received an e-mail about a huge scandal and been asked to forward the e-mail to everyone you know? How about an e-mail warning you about a deadly contaminant in your favourite food? Or an e-mail telling a funny story that seems too good to be true?

I recently received an e-mail that made my skin crawl! It also made me think twice before
5 buying a new down-filled duvet.

---

(1) My brother's girlfriend recently bought a down-filled duvet from a local discount store. The duvet seemed to be good quality and was a **steal of a deal**. She quickly replaced her old duvet with the new one. When she came back to the master bedroom about an hour later, the duvet had fallen halfway off the bed. Without a second thought, she straightened it out and went on with her day.

That night, she slept under the duvet and in the morning found it had again fallen to the floor. Finally, she cut open the duvet and was horrified to find that it was filled with **maggots**, because the **feathers** hadn't been cleaned properly!

These duvets are made in China, and they are sold at a price that is too good to be true. So, be warned: it's better to pay a bit more and go with a brand you trust than watch your purchase walk off the bed.

Forward this e-mail to everyone in your address book.

The e-mail came from a friend of mine and I knew she didn't have a brother, so right away I found it **suspect**. I quickly sent her an e-mail back asking for clarification. She told me that the e-mail had been forwarded to her from an acquaintance who did have a brother, but she didn't know the person very well either.

10 I did a bit more research and found that this story was complete fiction! I asked my friend how many people she had sent the e-mail to. Twenty-four. I contacted the person that sent her the original e-mail and asked her the same question. Twelve. Of the thirty-six people who had received the e-mail, I was the only one they knew of who had actually researched to see if it was true or not!

15 I began to realize how easily and how quickly these urban legends can make their way through cyberspace. I also began keeping track of forwarded e-mails and checking their validity. Here are two more that I personally received:

---

(2) Last week, Liza Lott, a mother in Florida, took her young son to McDonald's. After lunch, she let her son play in the play area outside. She watched him go straight to the ball pit, his favourite place, and play in the balls there. Five minutes later, he came back and said his leg hurt. His mother rubbed it a bit and took him home. Back home, his mother noticed some red marks on his leg, which she thought must be insect bites. An hour later, the boy was dead. It was discovered that the bites were snake bites. At the restaurant, they discovered a nest of rattlesnakes living in the ball pit, under the balls. So take care when you let your children play in outside play areas.

▶

③ BABY CARROTS **SOAKED** IN CHLORINE! Baby carrots are actually machine cut from **crooked** larger carrots and are then soaked in chlorinated water to give them a longer **shelf life**. If you are eating baby carrots, you are at risk of consuming high levels of chlorine! Buy large carrots and cut them yourself! Pass this on to everyone you know!!!

While the first two stories are completely false, the third does have some truth to it. Some baby carrots are cut from larger, irregular carrots. Also, according to the Canadian Food
20 Inspection Agency, the use of chlorine is common with fresh cut vegetables and there is also an acceptable level of chlorine that can be used. I don't know about you, but I'm not excited that my veggies are taking a dip in the pool before they meet my plate!

The next time you get a forwarded e-mail that sounds suspect, take a moment to verify if it's true or not. You can do a simple Internet search by copying and pasting a section of the
25 e-mail into your search engine. There are many websites that are dedicated to bringing you the truth! It's important to check the validity of an e-mail before sending it on to the people in your address book.

● **After you read, complete the chart with information from the text.**

Elements of the story which sound believable	Elements of the story which sound made up
Story 1 Maggots in the Duvet *- Getting a very good price on a usually expensive item*	
Story 2 Snakes in the Ball Pit	
Story 3 Chlorinated Carrots	

7 Liar, liar, pants on fire!

The beauty of urban legends is that they are just close enough to the truth that it can be difficult to tell if they are true or not. How good are you at telling an innocent lie?

- Read the example Speaking Card below. One story is true and two are false.

- Complete each of the speaking cards with one story that is true and two that are false.

- In a small group or as a class, read each of your stories out loud. Make notes on the stories your partners tell. Write down possible questions you could ask.

- Ask the storyteller yes/no questions about the stories. The first person to guess the true story wins a point. If no one can guess, then the storyteller wins the point.

- Have fun and don't take yourself too seriously!

Speaking Card: Describe something unexpected that happened today.

Story 1: *I was sitting in a café when a shoe came through the window and hit me on the head.*

Story 2: *I was sitting on a park bench when a man came up to me and splashed me with a bucket of cold water.*

Story 3: *I was walking around the museum when a woman came up to me and kissed me on the mouth.*

Speaking Card 1: Describe a time you got into an argument with someone.

Story 1: _____

_____

_____

Story 2: _____

_____

_____

Story 3: _____

_____

_____

Smart Talk

We were arguing about …

I was (furious / so angry / mad) because …

I was trying to explain that …

I thought my friend was being …

Notes: _____

Smart **Talk**

We were enjoying our vacation when …
We took a vacation to …
The funniest / scariest thing was …
First … then …

Notes: _____

Speaking Card 2: Describe something that happened to you while on vacation.

Story 1: _____
_____
_____

Story 2: _____
_____
_____

Story 3: _____
_____
_____

Speaking Card 3: Describe a time when you were completely surprised by something or someone.

Story 1: _____
_____
_____

Story 2: _____
_____
_____

Story 3: _____
_____
_____

Smart **Talk**

I was in shock / awe because …
It was so unexpected because …
I wasn't expecting … because …

Notes: _____

Smart **Talk**

It was in the evening / middle of the night and …
It was dark / late …
I thought I saw / heard …
I was walking / sitting … when …

Notes: _____

Speaking Card 4: Describe a time when you were scared by something or someone.

Story 1: _____
_____
_____

Story 2: _____
_____
_____

Story 3: _____
_____
_____

FINAL TASK

C3 8 Write and publish your own urban legend.

Write an urban legend and choose a method to pass it around. Maybe your story will go viral and become urban legend history.

STEP 1 Prepare

- Decide if you will use the plan you made on page 162 or if you will start a new story.
- If you are starting a new story, you will need to follow the steps on page 162 and write a new plan.
- Reread your plan and add or change any details before you begin writing.

STEP 2 Write

- Write the first draft of your story.
- Include at least one example of the past progressive tense and intensifiers.

  Start by writing the introduction paragraph. Remember that the introduction paragraph introduces the main characters and the setting and in urban legends often begins with a FOAF:

Last week I received an e-mail saying that … A friend of a friend of mine was walking down the street when …

_____
_____
_____
_____
_____

Next, create your body paragraphs, which will be the rising action in your story. Use the ideas from your plan. Add as much detail as you can. You may want to divide the rising action into more than one paragraph. Make a note in your rough copy of where the paragraph breaks will be.

The two young kids were playing with a hose and … The child was watching the microwave and …

_____
_____
_____
_____
_____

▶ _____
_____
_____
_____
_____
_____
_____
_____
_____
_____
_____

The poor dog exploded all over the inside of … Apparently, the child thought that if he put an animal in the microwave …

_____
_____
_____
_____
_____

STEP 3 Revise and Edit

- Reread your text. Have you included all the details to make your story complete?

- Check spelling and grammar. Did you use the past progressive tense correctly? Did you use intensifiers to make your story more interesting?

- Ask someone to look at your work and comment on it.

Name of the person who reviewed my text:

_____

Comments and suggestions: _____

_____
_____

STEP 4 Publish

- Write the final version of your story.

- Decide how you want to circulate your story (e-mail, word of mouth, public reading, …).

WRAP-UP

Try an extra activity using vocabulary from this unit on the Companion Website.

Test Your **Smarts**

Is it true that our brain can retain seven pieces of information easily? Can you remember more than seven Smart Words?

- Take two minutes to look at the Smart Words from this unit below and then cover them up.
- Write as many as you can remember in the chart.
- Then, work with a partner to see who can remember the most definitions of the words.

believable
reliable
crispy
bristle
go viral
maggot
feather
suspect
soaked
crooked
shelf life
swear
no frills
persist
tan
hook

Words	Definitions

Smart Expressions

- Read the definitions of the follow expressions.

  When you **spin a tale**, you tell a story.

  When you **bite your tongue**, you don't say what you are thinking.

  To **take someone for a ride** is to trick or deceive someone.

- Use each expression once to complete the paragraph.

  Mike loves to make fun of me. He starts by _____ that is so ridiculous I know

  he is _____. I always _____ as I listen.

GRAMMAR WORKSHOP 6.1

Intensifiers

What do you know?

Do you know how to use intensifiers?

Example: The family is **fabulously** wealthy.

- Underline the intensifiers.
- Check your answers at the bottom of the page.

  Example: Mr. Pitt told me the sewers are full of <u>extremely</u> large crocodiles.

  1. I was fairly sure that the story was untrue.

  2. Kim was totally confused by the e-mail she received.

  3. Terence is extremely careful about which e-mails he forwards to friends.

  4. Tash was very concerned when she heard that the story was true.

  5. Philip is definitely the master at creating urban legends.

  Score: _____/5

Rules

- Review the rules for using intensifiers in the chart below.

Intensifiers		
What are they?		
● Intensifiers are adverbs that modify (enhance) other adverbs and adjectives.		
Position	Intensifiers	Example
Place intensifiers in front of the adverbs or adjectives they modify.	too totally very extremely really definitely fairly relatively rather absolutely little	Mr. Tom, our English teacher, is **really** good at telling stories. (**really** modifies the adjective **good**) Rumours spread **very** quickly. (**very** modifies the adverb **quickly**) I was **extremely** happy when it was all over. (**extremely** modifies the adjective **happy**)

Answers: 1-fairly; 2-totally; 3-extremely; 4-very; 5-definitely

Practice

Exercise 1

● **Rewrite each sentence positioning the intensifiers correctly.**

Example: (extremely) This story is graphic.
This story is extremely graphic.

1. (really) Barb took the time to research the origins of the story.

_____

2. (totally) Mr. Kim was impressed with our hard work on the project.

_____

_____

3. (fairly / definitely) Mike's story was short and uninteresting.

_____

4. (very) This unit was interesting and fun.

_____

5. (rather) It seems odd that we couldn't find a good source for this story.

_____

_____

6. (really) The story Greg told was gory and disgusting.

_____

Exercise 2

● **Answer the questions, adding the intensifier in parentheses.**

Example: Was there a stiff breeze? (very)
There was a very stiff breeze.

1. Is Jane is a convincing storyteller? (very)

_____

2. Did Collin retell the urban legend well? (quite)

_____

3. Did Sandy choose a dark urban legend? (rather)

_____

4. Was Christina right about the story? (absolutely)

_____

5. Did Angelo present a unique urban legend. (totally)

_____

6. Is Bill is used to receiving e-mails about missing children? (relatively)

_____

Exercise 3

- Write a short paragraph describing someone you know using at least two intensifiers.

_____

_____

_____

_____

_____

_____

GRAMMAR WORKSHOP 6.2

Past Progressive Tense

What do you know?

Do you know how to use the past progressive tense?

Example: The cat **was waiting** at the mouse hole when the dog attacked.

- Decide if the sentence is in the simple past (SP) or past progressive (PP).
- Underline the verb(s) in the sentence.
- Check your answers at the bottom of the page.

	Simple Past	Past Progressive
Example: Nancy <u>told</u> us an urban legend.	✓	
❶ Jim read an urban legend that said Paul McCartney died in 1966.		
❷ Serena was listening to scary urban legends during a thunderstorm.		
❸ Walter didn't believe Sally's story about her uncle's cat.		
❹ Terissa was trying to come up with an urban legend to put on the Internet.		
❺ Tim and Alan were researching urban legends about food contamination over the weekend.		

Score: _____/5

Answers: 1-read, said, died, SP; 2-was listening, PP; 3-didn't believe, SP; 4-was trying, PP; 5-were researching, PP

Rules

● Review the rules for using verbs in the past progressive tense in the chart below.

Past Progressive Tense
When do you use it?
● To describe an action that took place in the past during a specific time frame
● To describe an action that was taking place when something else happened or while something else was happening

*Yesterday I **was talking** to my teacher when a journalist came into the classroom.* (action in progress)

Rule	Example
Subject + *to be* (past tense) + main verb + *–ing*	Gus **was** work**ing** when the power went out.

Key words: during, when, while, all night, all day

Tips
● Choose the simple past tense for actions that began and ended at a specific time in the past.
● Choose the past progressive tense for actions that took place during a specific period of time in the past.
Hint: When in doubt, use the simple past tense.

COMPANION **web+** Try extra grammar exercises for the past progressive tense on the Companion Website.

Practice

Exercise 1

● **Complete the sentences by circling the correct form of the verb: simple past or past progressive.**

Example: While Annie (worked /(was working)) on her homework, an e-mail arrived saying she had won a special prize.

1. Louis (told / was telling) us a story when the lights went out.

2. Police heard that people (received / were receiving) letters from around the world.

3. The letters (asked / were asking) the recipients to send money.

4. It (shocked / was shocking) Sally, because she had received a letter like the one in Louis' story.

5. When we (learned / were learning) that criminals (sent / were sending) fraudulent letters around the world, we were amazed.

6. While the police (investigated / were investigating) the stories in the letters, they (uncovered / were uncovering) hundreds of cases of fraud.

Exercise 2

- Complete each sentence using the past progressive.

- Circle any key words.

    Example: Wild rumours (circulate, already) _____**were already circulating**_____
    (when) the police announced that the photos were doctored.

1. While Stephanie (wait) _____ to receive a check
for millions from the Congo, she learned the story was false.

2. The people in the Congo (ask) _____ her
every week for more money for processing fees.

3. The e-mail was a scam, and she (go, never) _____
to receive any money.

4. I (wonder) _____ what the truth really
was when he told me the story.

5. All week she (make) _____ plans to send
the money, and then she heard the story was in fact a scam.

Exercise 3

- Write three sentences each in the simple past tense and the past
progressive tense using the affirmative, negative and question forms.

Simple Past

Affirmative: _**He finished his urban legend on the weekend.**_____

Negative: _**He didn't finish his urban legend on the weekend.**_____

Question: _**Did he finish his urban legend on the weekend?**_____

1. Affirmative: _____

Negative: _____

Question: _____

2. Affirmative: _____

Negative: _____

Question: _____

3. Affirmative: _____

Negative: _____

Question: _____

Past Progressive

Affirmative: _**John was writing his urban legend that day.**_____

Negative: _**John wasn't writing his urban legend that day.**_____

Question: _**Was John writing his urban legend that day?**_____

1. Affirmative: _____

Negative: _____

Question: _____

2. Affirmative: _____

Negative: _____

Question: _____

3. Affirmative: _____

Negative: _____

Question: _____

Exercise 4

- **Complete each sentence by underlining the correct verb forms.**
- **Circle any key words.**

Example: I (<u>saw</u> / was seeing) the man with the hook outside the car.

1. My friend Amy (received / was receiving) several strange calls while she (babysat / was babysitting) last night.

2. She (was / was being) too scared to leave the house afterward.

3. While the baby (slept / was sleeping), Amy (did / was doing) her homework.

4. Last night, I (read / was reading) a book about urban legends.

5. One story said that a babysitter (watched / was watching) television when the telephone (rang / was ringing) and the baby (went / was going) missing.

6. Between Saturday and Sunday, Jim (worked / was working) on a story about a babysitter and he (had / was having) several great ideas.

7. The man (sat / was sitting) in the car the whole time.

8. Maybe someone (tried / was trying) to play a trick on her during the evening. It (worked / was working) very well.

Exercise 5

- **Write your own paragraph explaining a scary moment in your life.**
- **Use the simple past and past progressive tenses.**

_____

_____

_____

_____

_____

_____

_____

_____

READING WORKSHOP 6

Using Character and Story Maps

In this workshop you will read a story about an urban legend. In order to understand the story you will practise an important strategy: using character maps and story maps.

– Character maps: This kind of map helps you to understand a story's main characters in more depth.

– Story maps: Use this map to help keep track of the events in a story, their causes and the outcome.

Before You Read

● Scan the story of an urban legend on page 180 and circle the names of the characters.

While You Read

● Fill in the story map with the important elements of the story.

Story Map
Main character(s)

Names _____ _____ _____	Descriptions _____ _____ _____

Setting

Where _____	When _____

Problem
Cecile dies. Jeremiah thinks she is still alive. Nobody believes him and they bury Cecile.

Events

Event 1 _Cecile falls into a coma_ and then dies. _____ _____ _____	Event 2 _____ _____ _____ _____	Event 3 _____ _____ _____ _____

Outcome
_____ _____

Urban Legend: Buried Alive

1 This is a story that has been in my family for many years. My grandfather told it to my father, who told it to me. He says it happened to his great-great-grandfather, Jeremiah Goodlife.

Jeremiah lived in Cardiff, Wales in the United Kingdom. He was a solicitor
5 or lawyer. He married my great-great-grandmother, Cecile, in 1814 when he was twenty-one and she was nineteen. They had been married for eighteen years when Cecile suddenly became **ill** with a fever. The doctor came but there was nothing he could do to help her.

For several days my great-grandmother lay in a coma. Jeremiah stayed by
10 her side. He helped to wash her face and tried to get her to **swallow** food. He never left her bedroom but slept and ate there himself. Everyone says that he was devoted to Cecile.

One night, Cecile seemed to stop breathing. Jeremiah immediately sent for the doctor. The doctor took one look at Cecile and told Jeremiah that
15 Cecile had died. Jeremiah couldn't believe it. He became very angry and sent the doctor away. Finally though, his children talked to him and got him to leave Cecile's room and get some rest.

Everyone believed that Cecile was dead. Everyone except my grandfather. Right up until the day of the funeral, my grandfather stayed in the room
20 with Cecile's body, insisting that she was just sleeping, not dead.

In those days they didn't have the same scientific methods that we have today. When someone died, they simply washed and dressed the body, put it in the coffin and buried it in the local churchyard.

Finally the day of the funeral came. Jeremiah's family took Cecile's coffin
25 and brought it to the church and then, to the graveyard. Just as they were about to lower the coffin into the ground, Jeremiah stood up and shouted, "She's not really dead! Open the coffin!" They had to take him away screaming and shouting while they buried Cecile.

That same night, Jeremiah dreamed that Cecile was alive in her coffin.
30 He dreamed that she was screaming and trying to **scratch** open the lid. The next morning he went to see the priest and the doctor but they refused to dig her up.

Jeremiah had this dream every night for a week. Every day he went to see the priest and the doctor begging them to **exhume** the body. Finally
35 the priest agreed even though he thought Jeremiah had lost his mind.

When Cecile's coffin was finally brought out of the ground and opened, everyone was shocked and horrified: Cecile was dead, but her eyes were wide open and her nails and hands were torn. The inside of the coffin was covered in scratches. She had been buried alive!

Smart Words

ill: sick

swallow: consume, eat, ingest

scratch: scrape or cut with fingers

exhume: take a dead body out of the ground

After You Read

- Fill in this character map of the main character, Jeremiah.

Character Map		
General information about Jeremiah	What Jeremiah says and does	What other people say or think about Jeremiah
• *Lawyer* _____ _____ _____ _____	• *He stays with his wife when she is sick.* _____ _____ _____ _____	• *Everyone says that he was devoted to Cecile.* _____ _____ _____ _____

- Answer these questions using the story map and the character map.

1. Why didn't anyone believe Jeremiah?

   _____

   _____

   _____

2. What qualities do you admire in Jeremiah?

   _____

   _____

   _____

3. What more could Jeremiah have done to save Cecile?

   _____

   _____

   _____

- Compare yourself with Jeremiah.

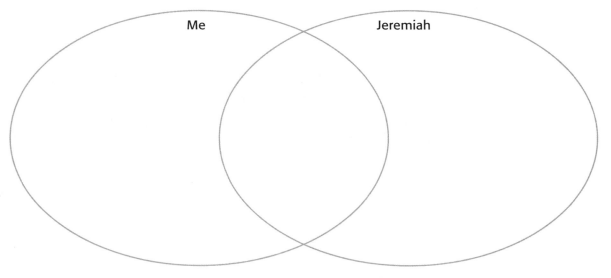

Me   Jeremiah

WRITING WORKSHOP ⑥

Short Story

A short story can be about imaginary or true events. Some are as short as a few paragraphs, others are many pages long. When you start writing a short story, it helps to visualize the entire story first so you can work out the chain of events that leads to the end.

Let's look at the features of a short story.

The plot of a short story includes an introduction (exposition), conflict, rising action, climax and resolution.

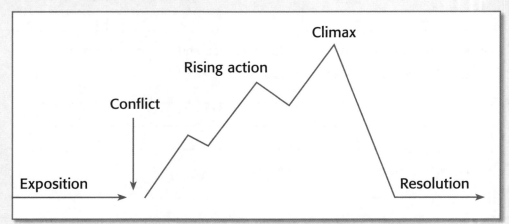

Introduction / Exposition

Short story writers typically introduce the main character and/or setting of the story at the very beginning. Here, their readers learn what they need to know to follow the story. For example, they may find out what happened before the story started. An introduction may include the following:

– **Characters:** their physical and personality traits

– **Background:** the main character's family, past experiences, job, and/or hobbies

– **Setting:** the time and place of the story

  • Time could mean time of day (morning, evening or night), the season (spring, summer, autumn or winter), or the year.

  • Place could mean a specific place (a house or a room, for instance), or a general place (for example, a ski slope or a beach).

- Underline the words that relate to a short story's characters.
- Circle the words that relate to a short story's setting.

<u>crazy</u>	teachers	from a poor family	(at dawn)	before going to bed
strict	in London	ninety-two years old	on a summer day	in a tent

- Read the introduction to a short story about an urban legend.
- List the main character(s), the place, the time and anything that already hints at what the story could be about.

A Dark and Stormy Night

This is a true story. Really. It happened on a road in northern Ontario about ten years ago. I heard about it on a newscast.

There was this guy hitchhiking across Canada to Alberta to get a job. He's waiting for a lift, on the side of the road, on a dark and stormy night. It's late November and it's raining hard. He can hardly see a few metres in front of him. He can't see any cars.

Who?	Where?	When?	What?

- Prepare to write a short story about an urban legend.
- Fill in the chart below with your choice of main character(s), a setting and what your urban legend might be about.

Who?	Where?	When?	What?
a teenage girl	*small cottage deep in Québec's countryside*	*in the 1950s, at night, during a snow storm*	*She could hear the doorbell ring again and again. Who could it be?*
_____	_____	_____	_____

Conflict

A story is not very interesting if everything goes well! A short story revolves around the main character. Something happens to this person. Perhaps he or she creates or encounters an obstacle. A conflict of some kind develops. A problem must be resolved.

- **Underline the first hint of a problem encountered by the main character in "A Dark and Stormy Night."**

Just as he thinks he's going to have to wait forever, a car pulls up beside him.

Without hesitation, the guy jumps in the car and slams the door. He turns to

thank the driver—but there's nobody behind the wheel!

- **Underline your choice of a major event that might affect your character or write your own.**

Your character

1. has an accident.

2. forgets something.

3. hears bad news.

4. sees something strange in a house.

5. gets sick.

6. Another event: _____

Rising action

What happens next? Usually a series of events happen as the main character tries to solve a problem or conflict that is developing.

- **Underline the most important event that occurs in the paragraph below.**

He looks out at the pouring rain and then at the empty seat beside him.

He can't decide. The car begins to drive slowly through the storm. The guy sees

a corner ahead. But the car doesn't slow down. Suddenly, just before the car hits

the corner, a hand sticks through the window, grabs the wheel and steers the

car around it.

- **Imagine another event in your urban legend.**
- **Brainstorm what this might be.**

_____

_____

_____

_____

Climax

Here the tension of the short story builds to its greatest intensity. Something happens to break the tension. It could be a fight or a major decision that means life or death for the character. Perhaps someone reveals a secret or a mystery gets solved.

- **Underline any words below that could relate to the climax of a story.**

  a fight   a walk in the park   a nap   an important decision

  a death   an ultimatum   a pause

- **Brainstorm what could happen at the climax of your urban legend.**

  _____

  _____

  _____

Resolution

After the conflict is resolved in the climax, the story comes to a close. Maybe the characters return home or they move on to new adventures. Whatever happens, it could be sad or happy.

- **Brainstorm what could happen to your characters.**

  _____

  _____

- **Read "A Dark and Stormy Night" from beginning to end.**

- **Identify all the elements of the plot: introduction, conflict, rising action, climax and resolution. Write them in the margin next to the text.**

Smart **Words**

slam: shut hard and loudly

steer: guide

A Dark and Stormy Night

1   This is a true story. Really. It happened on a road in northern Ontario about ten years ago. I heard about it on a newscast.

Introduction

There was this guy hitchhiking across Canada to Alberta to get a job. He's waiting for a lift, on the side of the road, on a dark and stormy night.
5   It's late November and it's raining hard. He can hardly see a few metres in front of him. He can't see any cars.

Just as he thinks he's going to have to wait forever, a car pulls up beside him. Without hesitation, the guy jumps in the car and **slams** the door. He turns to thank the driver—but there's nobody behind the wheel!

10   He looks out at the pouring rain and then at the empty seat beside him. He can't decide. The car begins to drive slowly through the storm. The guy sees a corner ahead. But the car doesn't slow down. Suddenly, just before the car hits the corner, a hand sticks through the window, grabs the wheel and **steers** the car around it.

▶

▶

15 Stunned, the guy can't move. The car keeps going, driverless. Just as he begins to catch his breath, another curve appears and then the hand, steering the car to safety. This happens twice more. By now our guy's **heart is in his throat**. The car pulls to a stop beside a bar on the **outskirts** of some town. The guy throws open the door and jumps out.

20 Soaked and trembling, he hurries into the bar. He slaps down some change on the counter and demands a drink. He begins telling anybody who will listen what just happened. A silence falls as the patrons realize this guy is serious: he's crying hysterically and he isn't drunk. A few minutes later, two other guys run in. They stop abruptly when they see our guy. One of them

25 says to the other, "Hey, Badou, there's that crazy guy who got in our car while we were pushing it!"

Smart Words

heart is in the throat: really anxious

outskirts: area bordering a town

It's Your Turn

- Write a short story about an urban legend using the notes you took above.

- Imagine your audience is a group of teenagers.

- Use the past progressive and as many intensifiers as possible.

  Here are tips for writing your urban legend:
  - Make your urban legend seem as plausible as possible.
  - Think of the five senses as you write: What do your characters see, hear, touch, taste or smell?
  - Think ahead to a possible ending as you write.

- Write a title. _____

- Write the first line of your introduction. Here are some suggestions.
  - *This is the story of a teenager …*
  - *It happened to my girlfriends …*
  - *Thomas was a serious man …*
  - Invent your own first line: _____

    _____

- Write the rest of your introduction. Remember:

  1. Introduce your main character(s).

  2. Describe the setting. Here are some suggestions.
     - *It was a hot day in July …*
     - *Outside the house, the snow never stopped falling …*
     - *There I was in my room, it was dawn …*

     _____
     _____
     _____
     _____
     _____
     _____

3. Write something that hints at what is going to happen.

_____

_____

_____

_____

_____

- Describe the chain of events that make up the rising action.

_____

_____

_____

_____

_____

_____

_____

_____

_____

_____

_____

_____

- Describe the climax. What happens finally? What is the "punch" of the story?

_____

_____

_____

_____

_____

_____

_____

_____

- Describe the resolution. How does the story end? Not every legend has a resolution. Sometimes it ends abruptly and the story finishes with the climax.

_____

_____

_____

_____

_____

_____

- Write the final version of your story on a separate piece of paper.

REFERENCE SECTION

Table of Contents

Verb Tenses

Simple Present Tense

When do you use it?
- For repeated actions or routines: I **sing** for my supper every evening.
- For facts, opinions and general truths: I think she **sings** beautifully.

Affirmative	
Rule	Examples
Add *s* to the base form of the verb for the third person singular.	I **sing**. He / She / It **sings**. We / You / They **sing**.
Add *–es* for words ending in *–sh, –ch, –s, –z, –x* and *–o*.	She **watches** the clock.

Negative (contraction)	
Rule	Examples
Add *do not* (*don't*) or *does not* (*doesn't*) before the verb.	I **do not** (**don't**) **sing**. He **does not** (**doesn't**) **sing**. We **do not** (**don't**) **sing**.

Question	
Rule	Examples
Start the question with *do* or *does*.	**Do** I **sing**? **Does** she **sing**? **Do** they **sing**?

Exceptions	
Verb *to have*	Verb *to be*
I **have** (I've) He / She / It **has** We / You / They **have**	I **am** (I'm) You **are** (You're) He / She / It **is** (He's / She's / It's) We / They **are** (We're / They're)

Key words: every day, often, usually, all the time, sometimes, never

Present Progressive Tense

When do you use it?
- To describe an action taking place right now: He **is playing** in the band with his friends.
- To describe a definite event that will take place in the future: I **am playing** in the band tonight.

Affirmative	Negative
Subject + verb *to be* + infinitive + *ing* She **is** play**ing**.	Add *not* after the verb *to be*. She **is not** play**ing**.

Question	
Auxiliary verb *to be* + subject + *ing* (+ key word) **Is** she play**ing** right now?	

Key words: right now, soon, today, tonight, at the moment, still

Simple Past Tense of Regular Verbs

When do you use it?

● For actions that began and ended in the past.

Affirmative	Negative (contraction)	Question
Add –*ed* to the end of the verb:	Add *did not* (or the contraction *didn't*) before the verb:	Add *did* before the subject:
I watch**ed** the movie.	I **did not** (**didn't**) watch the movie.	**Did** I watch the movie?
You listen**ed** to the music.	You **did not** listen to the music.	**Did** you listen to the music?
She work**ed** hard.	He **did not** work hard.	**Did** she / he work hard?
We lik**ed** the film.	We **did not** like the film.	**Did** we like the film?
They talk**ed** in the library.	They **did not** talk in the library.	**Did** they talk in the library?

Key words: yesterday, last night, last week, last year

Simple Past Tense of the Verb *To Be*

Affirmative	Negative (contraction)	Question
I **was**	I **was not** (**wasn't**)	**Was** I?
You **were**	You **were not** (**weren't**)	**Were** you?
She / He / It **was**	She / He / It **was not** (**wasn't**)	**Was** she / he / it?
We **were**	We **were not** (**weren't**)	**Were** we?
You **were**	You **were not** (**weren't**)	**Were** you?
They **were**	They **were not** (**weren't**)	**Were** they?

Simple Past Tense of Irregular Verbs

Use the Irregular Verbs List on page 199 of the Reference Section.

Affirmative	Negative (contraction)	Question
I **began** to write.	I **did not** (**didn't**) **begin** to write.	**Did** I **begin** to write?
You **felt** happy.	You **did not feel** happy.	**Did** you **feel** happy?
He **heard** the music.	She **did not hear** the music.	**Did** he / she **hear** the music?
We **ate** lunch.	We **did not eat.**	**Did** we **eat**?
They **had** a discussion.	They **did not have** a discussion.	**Did** they **have** a discussion?

Past Progressive Tense

When do you use it?

● To describe an action taking place during a specific time: I **was sleeping** between midnight and ten a.m.
● To describe an action that was taking place in the past when it was interrupted by another action: He **was walking** to school when a snowball hit him.

Do not use the past progressive for past habits: I **used** to believe in ghosts.

Do not use the past progressive for past facts or generalizations: My teacher **taught** us about ghosts.

Affirmative	Negative	Question
Subject + *was/were* + verb + *ing*	Add *not* after the verb *to be*.	Put the auxiliary verb *to be* first.
They **were dancing**.	They **were not dancing**.	**Were** they **dancing** when you saw them?

Key words: while, during, between … and …, when … happened, all night, all day

Future Tense

When do you use it?

- To express a prediction: Luc **is going to pass** his exam. Matéo **will win** the science fair.
- To express a plan: Julie **is going to learn** to drive.
- To express an intention: Janet **will study** for her test.

Affirmative

Subject	+	*will*	+	base form of verb	+	rest of sentence.
I		**will**		**walk**		to school today.

Subject	+	verb *to be*	+	*going to*	+	base form of verb	+	rest of sentence.
I		**am**		**going to**		**walk**		to school today.

Negative (contraction)

Subject	+	*will not / won't*	+	base form of verb	+	rest of sentence.
I		**will not / won't**		**walk**		to school today.

Subject	+	verb *to be*	+	*not*	+	*going to*	+	base form of verb	+	rest of sentence.
I		**am**		**not**		**going to**		**walk**		to school today.

Question

Will	+	subject	+	base form of the verb	+	rest of sentence.
Will		you		**walk**		to school today?

Verb *to be*	+	subject	+	*going to*	+	base form of verb	+	rest of sentence.
Are		you		**going to**		**walk**		to school today?

Key words: tomorrow, later, next week, next year, today

Imperative

When do you use it?

- To give an order: **Be** quiet!
- To give a warning or advice: **Watch** your step.
- To make a request: Please **help** me.
- To give directions: **Turn** right at the light.

Affirmative

Use the infinitive of the verb but drop the *to*:

Come here now!   **Be** careful!   **Sit** down.   **Keep** going straight.

Negative (contraction)

Add *do not* or *don't* before the verb:

Don't talk back!   **Do not walk** on the grass.   **Don't go!**   **Don't stop!**

Modals		
Function	Modal auxiliary	Examples
To express possibility	may / might	She **may** be absent from gym class. I **might** be able to come for dinner.
To express capability	can / could	You **could** run very fast when you were young.
To express permission	may / can	**Can** I forward this e-mail?
To be polite	would / could	**Would** you please pass me the salt? **Could** you please be quiet?
To give advice	should	She **should** stop smoking. My brother **should** study more.
To express obligation	must / have to	You **mustn't** drive so fast. You **have to** stop shopping so much.
To express an intention or promise	will	I **will** try to stop.

Questions

Yes/No Questions						
There are two ways to form yes/no questions.						
Verb *to be*	+ subject	+ adjective	= answer			
Are	you	bilingual?	Yes, I am.			
Is	your mother	American?	No, she isn't.			
Auxiliary	+ subject	+ verb	+ rest of question	= answer		
Do	you	understand	Chinese?	No, I don't.		
Does	she	speak	Greek?	Yes, she does.		

Information Questions						
There are two ways to form information questions using question words.						
Question word	+ verb *to be*	+ rest of question				
What	are	coins?				
Where	is	Australia?				
Question word	+ verb *to be*	+ subject	+ verb	+ rest of question		
Where	do	you	want	to travel?		
Why	does	the teacher	speak	so quickly?		

Question Word	Refers to	Example
Who?	A person	**Who** speaks English?
What?	An object, a thing, a name	**What** city do you want to visit?
Where?	A place	**Where** do you live?
When?	A time or a date	**When** were you born?
Why?	A reason	**Why** do you like to speak English?
Whose?	A possession or belonging	**Whose** bag is this?
Which?	A choice	**Which** city do you prefer?
How?	A way, a manner	**How** do you get to school?

How can be used together with many adjectives: How far? How big? How long? How many?

How many is used for things you can count (friends, desks, people): How many video games do you have?

How much is used for things you can't count (sugar, coffee, money): How much money do you have?

Count and Non-Count Nouns

Count Nouns		

Most nouns in English are count nouns. This means that they can be counted. To form the plural of a count noun, add the letter **s** alone or with other letters as follows.

Noun category	Forming the plural	Example
Most nouns	Add s	car ⟶ car**s**
Nouns ending in –x, –ch –sh, –s, –z	Add es	class ⟶ class**es**
Nouns ending in –f, –fe	Change f to v + add es or s	half ⟶ hal**ves**
Nouns ending in a consonant + –y	Change y to i + add es	butterfly ⟶ butterfl**ies**
Nouns ending in a consonant + –o	Add es	echo ⟶ echo**es**

Exceptions					

Some count nouns have an irregular plural form:

Singular	Plural	Singular	Plural	Singular	Plural
aircraft	aircraft	fish	fish	ox	oxen
axis	axes	foot	feet	person	people
bacterium	bacteria	formula	formulae/formulas	phenomenon	phenomena
cactus	cacti	fungus	fungi	series	series
child	children	goose	geese	sheep	sheep
crisis	crises	man	men	species	species
criterion	criteria	moose	moose	tooth	teeth
deer	deer	mouse	mice	woman	women

Non-Count Nouns			

Some nouns are *always* considered singular. They are called non-count nouns because they cannot be counted.

Category	Examples	Category	Examples
Groups of objects	equipment, furniture, hair	Fluids	milk, gasoline, water
Masses	rice, sand, sugar	Abstract ideas	happiness, love, sadness

Adjectives

Adjectives		

When do you use them?
- To describe nouns: Carl is a **nice** guy.
- To compare two or more nouns by using the equivalent (same), the comparative or the superlative forms.
- For the equivalent form, use *as … as*: **as** small **as**, **as** pale **as**, **as** big **as**.

Simple	Comparative	Superlative
For one-syllable adjectives that end in a consonant For one-syllable adjectives that end in consonant / vowel / consonant	add *–er + than*: small ⟶ small**er than** add a consonant + *–er*: big ⟶ bigg**er than** thin ⟶ thinn**er than**	add *the* + adjective + *–est*: **the** small**est** add *the* + adjective + consonant + *est*: **the** bigg**est**
For adjectives ending in *–e*	add *–r*: simple ⟶ simple**r than** wise ⟶ wise**r than**	add *the* + adjective + *st*: **the** simpl**est**

Simple	Comparative	Superlative
For one- or two-syllable adjectives ending in *–y*	change the *y* to *i* + *–er + than*: crazy ⟶ craz**ier than** busy ⟶ bus**ier than**	use *the* + adjective, then change the *y* to *i* + *–est*: **the** craz**iest** **the** bus**iest**
For two-syllable adjectives that do <u>not</u> end in *–y*	use *more/less* + adjective + *than*: extreme ⟶ **more** extreme **than** awesome ⟶ **less** awesome **than**	use *the most / the least* + adjective: **the most** extreme **the least** awesome
For adjectives with three or more syllables	use *more/less* + adjective + *than*: dangerous ⟶ **more** dangerous **than** spectacular ⟶ **less** spectacular **than**	use *the most / the least* + adjective: **the most** dangerous **the least** spectacular

Exceptions		
good	better than	the best
bad	worse than	the worst
little	less than	the least
few	fewer than	the fewest
far	farther / further than	the farthest / the furthest

Adverbs

Adverbs	
An adverb is used to describe a verb: She writes **quickly**. Adverbs usually go *after* the verb in a sentence.	
Rule	Examples
To make an adverb, add *–ly* to the end of the adjective.	quiet ⟶ quiet**ly** beautiful ⟶ beautiful**ly** slow ⟶ slow**ly**
If the adverb ends in *–y*, change the *y* to *i* and add *–ly*.	happy ⟶ happ**ily** angry ⟶ angr**ily** lucky ⟶ luck**ily**

Pronouns and Possessive Adjectives

Pronouns and Possessive Adjectives				
Subject pronouns	Object pronouns	Reflexive pronouns	Possessive pronouns	Possessive adjectives
Acts as the subject	Acts as an object	Refers to the subject	Acts as a marker of possession and defines ownership	Indicates ownership
I you she/he/it we you they	me you her/him/it us you them	myself yourself herself/himself/itself ourselves yourselves themselves	mine yours hers/his ours yours theirs	my your her/his/its our your their
she saved my life.	She saved **me**.	He repaired it **himself**.	The book is **yours**.	It is **her** medal.

Articles

Indefinite Article: *A*	
When do you use it? Use the indefinite articles *a* and *an* when talking about nouns in a general, unspecific way.	
Rule	Example
Use an indefinite article in front of a singular count noun.	I see **a** carrot on the table.
Use an indefinite article in front of a profession.	She is **a** teacher.
Use an indefinite article when giving the rate or pace of something.	One gigabyte (GB) **a** second

Indefinite Article: *An*	
Rule	Examples
The indefinite article **an** is used in front of words that start with the vowels *a, e, i, o, u* or the silent *h* sound.	**an** apple **an** e-mail **an** old dog **an** hour

Definite Article: *The*	
When do you use it? Use the definite article ***the*** to talk about specific nouns.	
Rule	Examples
Use a definite article when discussing something already talked about.	Do you remember **the** e-mail I sent you?
Use a definite article when there is only one such thing or person in the world.	**the** Internet, **the** sky, **the** Earth
Use a definite article in front of an important title.	**the** Prime Minister of Canada
Use a definite article in front of names of newspapers, buildings, hotels.	**the** *Gazette*, **the** CN Tower, **the** Château Frontenac

Exceptions	
Do not use articles for:	Examples
Sports	I play soccer, basketball and rugby.
Unspecified, plural nouns	I love to eat strawberries.
Nouns that can't be counted (such as money, time, water, information)	We need money to buy information about water resources.
Most countries (unless their names contain a plural or they have an official title)	France, Great Britain, Canada, Australia, Spain; but **the** United States, **the** Republic of China, **the** Czech Republic

Prepositions

Prepositions			
Purpose	Preposition		Example
Direction	down from	to up	I drove home **from** Montréal. I'm walking **to** school.
Place	above against at behind between in	in front of inside on on top of under	The bird flies **above** the trees. My sister is **at** home. I don't want to sit **between** those two people. We live **in** a city. The paper is **in front of** you. My school is **on** Royal Avenue.
Time	at for	in on	I will meet you **at** six o'clock. We celebrate Valentine's Day **on** February 14.
Tip			

Two of the most easily confused prepositions are **to** and **at**:

- Use **to** to indicate movement from one place to another: I will walk **to** your house.
- Use **at** to indicate staying in one place: I am **at** school.

Connectives

Connectives		
When	Connectives	Examples
For cause and effect	because because of therefore consequently such … that so … that so that since due to so	People decided to get involved **because** the director's speech was so persuasive. **Because of** the delay, we cannot start the project. Humanitarian aid didn't arrive. **Therefore / Consequently**, people died. The weather is **so** bad **that** the roads are closed. The food bank is open seven days a week **so that** people in need can come any time.
Contrast of ideas	even though despite nevertheless although but however anyway	**Even though** it was a great initiative, it didn't work out. They raised a lot of money **despite** all the organizational problems. Thousands of people participated in the rally. **Nevertheless,** they didn't raise enough money. The fundraisers are disappointed, **but** they won't give up. **However**, they will try something different next time.
Conditions	otherwise or else	Fortunately the community gives to our local food bank. **Otherwise**, some people would go hungry. The children need school uniforms, **or else** they can't go to school.

Capitalization and Punctuation

Capitalization	
Category	Examples
Places (countries, cities, regions, lakes, etc.)	**M**exico, **L**ac **S**t-**J**ean, **B**rome **M**issisquoi
Events	the **O**lympics, **W**orld **A**ids **D**ay
Holidays and celebrations	**N**ew **Y**ear's **D**ay, **M**other's **D**ay
Languages and peoples	**S**panish, **O**jibwa, the **I**nuit
Organizations, departments and institutions	**T**oronto **P**olice **D**epartment, **M**c**G**ill **U**niversity
Planets, stars, galaxies	**E**arth, **M**ars, the **M**ilky **W**ay
Titles (Capitalize all words except articles, prepositions and short conjunctions; for example, *the, a, an, on, in, and, but, for, nor, or.*)	**L**ittle **R**ed **R**iding **H**ood, *C*atcher in the *R*ye, the **P**rime **M**inister of **C**anada

Punctuation		
Punctuation marks make a written message clearer. Using a punctuation mark (or forgetting it) can sometimes change the meaning of a sentence.		
Punctuation mark	Function	Examples
Period (**.**)	To finish a sentence	**We decided to form a band.**
Question mark (**?**)	To indicate a question	**How are you?**
Exclamation mark (**!**)	To indicate strong emotion	**I can't believe it!**
Comma (**,**)	• Between items in a list • To separate two phrases	**I need a book, a pen and a desk.** **Rachel, my girlfriend, is coming over.**
Apostrophe (**'**)	• In contractions • To show possession	**It's raining outside.** **Carl's mother called.**

Intensifiers

Intensifiers		
What are they?		
• Intensifiers are adverbs that modify (enhance) other adverbs and adjectives.		
Position	Intensifiers	Example
Place intensifiers in front of the adverbs or adjectives they modify.	too totally very extremely really definitely fairly relatively rather absolutely little	Mr. Tom, our English teacher, is **really** good at telling stories. (**really** modifies the adjective **good**) Rumours spread **very** quickly. (**very** modifies the adverb **quickly**) I was **extremely** happy when it was all over. (**extremely** modifies the adjective **happy**)

Irregular Verbs List

- Write a definition or translation for each verb.

Base Form	Simple Past	Past Participle	Definition:
1. awake	awoke	awoken	
2. be	was, were	been	
3. beat	beat	beaten	
4. become	became	become	
5. begin	began	begun	
6. bend	bent	bent	
7. bet	bet	bet	
8. bite	bit	bitten	
9. bleed	bled	bled	
10. break	broke	broken	
11. bring	brought	brought	
12. buy	bought	bought	
13. catch	caught	caught	
14. choose	chose	chosen	
15. come	came	come	
16. cut	cut	cut	
17. deal	dealt	dealt	
18. do	did	done	
19. draw	drew	drawn	
20. dream	dreamed, dreamt	dreamed, dreamt	
21. drink	drank	drunk	
22. drive	drove	driven	
23. eat	ate	eaten	
24. fall	fell	fallen	
25. feel	felt	felt	

▶

Base Form	Simple Past	Past Participle	Definition:
26. fight	fought	fought	
27. find	found	found	
28. fly	flew	flown	
29. forbid	forbade	forbidden	
30. forget	forgot	forgotten	
31. forgive	forgave	forgiven	
32. get	got	gotten, got	
33. give	gave	given	
34. go	went	gone	
35. grow	grew	grown	
36. have	had	had	
37. hear	heard	heard	
38. hit	hit	hit	
39. hold	held	held	
40. hurt	hurt	hurt	
41. keep	kept	kept	
42. know	knew	known	
43. learn	learned, learnt	learned, learnt	
44. leave	left	left	
45. lose	lost	lost	
46. make	made	made	
47. meet	met	met	
48. pay	paid	paid	
49. put	put	put	
50. read	read	read	
51. ride	rode	ridden	
52. run	ran	run	

Base Form	Simple Past	Past Participle	Definition:
53. say	said	said	
54. see	saw	seen	
55. sell	sold	sold	
56. send	sent	sent	
57. set	set	set	
58. shake	shook	shaken	
59. shine	shone	shone	
60. show	showed	showed, shown	
61. shut	shut	shut	
62. sing	sang	sung	
63. sit	sat	sat	
64. sleep	slept	slept	
65. slide	slid	slid	
66. smell	smelled, smelt	smelled, smelt	
67. speak	spoke	spoken	
68. speed	sped	sped	
69. spell	spelled, spelt	spelled, spelt	
70. spend	spent	spent	
71. stand	stood	stood	
72. take	took	taken	
73. teach	taught	taught	
74. tear	tore	torn	
75. tell	told	told	
76. think	thought	thought	
77. understand	understood	understood	
78. wear	wore	worn	
79. win	won	won	
80. write	wrote	written	

SPELLING LOG

When you misspell a word, write the mistake and the correction in your spelling log. Then check the log before you hand in a writing assignment.

Mistake	Correction

GRAMMAR LOG

When your teacher returns a writing assignment, identify your errors and write them in your grammar log. Then check the log when you edit your writing assignments.

PHOTO CREDITS

ALAMY

p. 33 (c): I. Kisselev

p. 33 (l): T. Bannor

p. 65 (l): S. Severino

p. 66: ACE STOCK LIMITED

p. 134: R. Adlercreutz

p. 137: B. Lewis

p. 147: Eye Ubiquitous

p. 148: The Art Archives

CORBIS

pp. x, 5: D. Stewart, Photex, zefa

p. 15: R. Holz, zefa

p. 44: R. Farris

p. 103: R. Friedman

p. 127 (b): A. Maher, Sygma

p. 127 (c): C. Morris

p. 127 (c, t): K. Ward

p. 127 (t): Bettmann

p. 138: C. Savage

COURTESY OF ADBUSTERS.ORG

p. 99

COURTESY OF JON STEIN

p. 8

CP IMAGES

p. 125

p. 127 (centre, bottom): F. Chartrand

ISTOCKPHOTO

p. 1 (b): O. Prikhodko

p. 34: A. Manley

p. 35: G. Barskaya

p. 65 (b, r): mayo5

p. 101: O. Graf, zefa

p. 152: C. Dewald

p. 155 (c): M. Scisetti

p. 157: B. Kosanovic

p. 165 (b): A. Nacu

NEWSCOM

p. 11: CHAMUSSY, SIPA

PHOTOTHÈQUE ERPI

p. 45

p. 106

p. 108

p. 129 (b)

SHUTTERSTOCK

p. iii Andresr

p. 1 (t, l): D. Cervo

p. 1 (t, r): J. Stitt

p. 2: photobank.kiev.ua

p. 13: Tumar

p. 16: Sint

p. 33 (r): Y. Arcurs

p. 40: A. Blazic

p. 46: MitarArt

p. 65 (t, r): L.Christensen

p. 67: Shots Studio

p. 70: AVAVA

p. 71: G. Detonnancourt

p. 75: Ayakovlev

p. 77: S. Miles

p. 78 M. Marcello

p. 90: Wrangler

p. 95 (c): paffy

p. 95 (l): J. AS Rayes

p. 95 (right): Beboy

p. 97: N. Mikhaylova

p. 129 (t): arindambanerjee

p. 155 (l): M. Antonino

p. 155 (r): C. Musat

p. 155 (t, r): ducu59us

p. 156: D. Mikhail

p. 160: Mcarper

p. 165 (t): J. Duplass

p. 167: B. Hofacker

p. 168: D. Green

p. 169 (b): A. Deanphotography

p. 169 (c): M. Antonino

p. 169 (t): oliveromg

p. 170: eurobanks

THOMAS VALLIÈRES

p. 130

Notes: _____

Notes: